Dear single self

A COLLECTION OF LETTERS FROM ALL OVER THE WORLD SPARKING COURAGE, WISDOM AND HOPE FOR WOMEN OVER 30 AND SINGLE.

AMANDA VIVIERS

DEAR SINGLE SELF
Amanda Viviers

First edition published 2016

Published in Western Australia

All enquiries regarding this publication and speaking engagements:

www.amandaviviers.com | info@amandaviviers.com
@authoramandaviviers

@amandaviviers

Book design by Kellie Parsons

kellie@kelliemaree.com | www.kelliemaree.com | @_kelliemaree_

Dedicated to my sister Jen.

You are faithful, You are kind and You are brilliant.

Foreward

Amanda Viviers – formerly Amanda Powell. I met this lady when she was a single, young, vibrant, creative, fast, relentless, passionate-about-supporting-people superwoman, with no potential partner in sight. My thoughts in those early years were – there wasn't much room in her days anyway, and the pickings were slim because there would be few who could run fast enough to catch her!

I loved this young woman immediately and was privileged to become a slightly older friend, confidant and mentor. What I discovered in this friendship was her desire to find a great guy who would be just as passionate about life and people as she was, could compliment her well, was kind, and would sing her 'life's song and calling' back to her in times when she felt stuck, in-between and had forgotten some of the melody.

This was her desire but I can tell you there were many times in those many, many years of her being single, and not wanting to be alone for yet another Christmas, that revealed the vulnerability of her humanness.

This is our humanness; to be connected, to be accepted, to love and be loved. However, we must remember that having a partner does not necessarily fill the void of loneliness. Our communities are full of lonely people, some living on their own and others living in a full house but who are desperately lonely because there is no love and no real connection.

Amanda wasn't lonely but she was single, and didn't want to be.

The biggest value I believe myself and some other slightly older friends, like Kelley, Rose and Sarah, brought to her single years was that we loved her, were good listeners, calming, gave a few 'tips and tricks' (couldn't help ourselves) but importantly we had the perspective of life and experienced partnerships. We were her mentor-friends. We knew that building a healthy life and partnership begins with a healthy you, and that it was critical to keep sure and pure to who you are but prepared that mutual compromises will come, and most importantly that even finding a great partner doesn't solve and heal all of our own personal insecurities.

Mentor-friendships with a few who are that little bit further down the track, have the ability to provide the strength, cheering up and skills for that hand-up when you are down and doubting your dreams, are priceless friendships.

Allow Amanda and the words on these pages to encourage, bring knowledge and provide strength for your days.

Penny Webb

Amanda's Friend!

Book chatter...

This book feels like the circle of older sisters I never had. Amanda has curated wise and witty voices to contribute stories of challenge, excitement and hope. It has strengthened and empowered me, as a single woman, to rejoice in exactly who and where I am.

Anna McGahan, Actress

You cannot read this book and remain passive; it will change your life if you allow it. There is much to learn from this collection of eloquently written stories by emotionally insightful women. They speak to the depth of longing and excitement, previously experienced as fear, and make a commitment to loving themselves unconditionally. Embody the journey of Dear Single Self and it may just lead you to greater compassion, joy and purpose.

Ann Galambosi, Psychologist

Everyone knows Amanda is inspiring. That leaps off the page. Those who have heard her know she's a brilliant communicator. But here's what I love most about Amanda: she loves well. And that impresses me more than anything else in life. People who love, especially those considered "least", well.

Jarrad Mckenna, Hand Model and Underwater Basket Weaver

This is a refreshingly original piece of reading that is much a reflection of the author; geared towards seeing others living out their life journeys with an encouraged revelation of self, hopeful, full of wisdom and perspective. This book is a creative adventure. A true blessing

Jo-Anne Hodges, Writer

The women of this book invited me warmly into the weird, exuberant, collective dance that is womanhood and, partnerless, I joined in. Their exhortations were so liberating that I spontaneously went out and got myself a daring new haircut. It was bad – I looked like a poodle – but I was free.

Alyshia Byrne, Writer

Amanda's writing has a way of tapping into the un-chartered areas of your heart and soul - engaging with those deeper, unsurfaced desires and questions that we so rarely give time and space for, in our rushed and productivity-driven lives.

This book shines light on such an important part of a woman's life, that is not given enough space to be heard or understood.

She sets the pace for a new-normal and a counter-approach to messages society sends single women. A very worthy read for any single woman.

Lauren Hack, Interior Designer

Amanda has a beautiful way of drawing authenticity out of others, and sharing her vulnerability with grace and courage. Reading her work is like sitting with a dear friend and talking over coffee. You come away feeling challenged and empowered.

Lizzy Milani, Writer, Speaker and Co- owner of Pocket Fuel

Dear Single Self" is more than a book for our 'single' selves. These letters could easily be addressed to our anxious selves, our perfectionist selves and our 'convinced-we're not enough selves'. In a world of voices telling us to strive harder, Amanda and friends whisper to those of us in our 20's, through stunning vulnerability and beautiful bravery, that just maybe it is all going to be ok.

Beth Bracegirdle, Writer, Journalist and Activist

Chapters

CHAPTER ONE

The summer of love

Long pants are in, aren't they?

Winter was waning and everyone around me was dusting off their picnic baskets, getting ready for summer to sing. It seemed like the whole city had gone to mush and become romance mad.

I wasn't interested in the slightest.

Well, maybe I was, but I wasn't willing to tell my sad story one more time as I sat at another function, surrounded by newly weds, lovers and old timers, telling me their three point sermons on how to get hitched!

Seriously, if one more person asked me to be their bridesmaid or gave me that sad look as they asked, "Are you still single?", I might just vomit.

The cold days faded slowly that year and I wished they could hang around longer. It would give me another excuse to stay in my flannelette pyjamas, eat chocolate and wear my Ugg boots all day, even to the local shops.

My favourite hero was Bridget Jones and her awkwardness made me feel somewhat normal. There I was in a flat for two, surrounded by lovely people and things, but extremely unhappy. I was a little overweight, spent a lot of time alone and had many unfulfilled dreams.

It was like I was waiting for the day to come where suddenly I would give myself permission to live life fully. The magic formula to living that life was me plus man (any man!) equalled my very firm picture of perfection.

I had kept dreaming of the day Jerry McGuire would say softly, "You complete me." I realised quickly that summer though, that,

Hollywood, you're a liar!

I worked like a maniac, filling every moment with my career, striving to find a sense of wholeness through my achievements.

I was over caffeinated,

affection starved,

exhausted,

and

dissatisfied.

Something had to change.

I needed to make brave steps towards the life I only dared to dream of.

I thought in that summer, the change I longed for would be my relationship status on Facebook, but instead I was in for an adventure that no-one could have predicted.

Especially not me.

I fell in love that summer. It was indeed the summer of love.

The person I fell in love with was not a man (that was to come much later). I fell in love with a thirty-something, woman who was sassy and bold, who was tender and kind, who was a little overweight, but beautiful just the same.

I fell in love with me.

I learnt how to go to the movies by myself and loved it.

I learnt how to buy a house and not wait for another signature on the bottom line.

I learnt how to holiday in far off places, loving life and moments without another sitting on the plane beside me.

It was in learning to love myself that I became available and open enough to learn to love another.

I had to give myself permission to truly live and the rest took care of itself.

I needed to date myself (weird I know!).

Welcome to the summer of love, a season of truly facing my single self and saying 'you are okay ... really okay'.

If I never found someone to call my own, I found a peace that surpassed understanding.

create a life that feels good on the inside
not just one that looks good on the outside

"Date yourself. Take yourself out to eat. Don't share your popcorn at the movies with anyone. Stroll around an art museum alone. Fall in love with canvases. Fall in love with yourself."

Anon

CHAPTER TWO

What this book is not ...

This book is not full of quick answers and easy fixes.

It is not a three-point sermon or a machine that you put your money into and out rolls a spouse.

It is not designed to give you answers; it has been designed to provoke questions. Hopefully questions that will bring radical life change.

Are in for that kind of messing up? Are you willing to go into this journey with an open mind and a contrite heart?

Then this is what I am suggesting: that you take time for yourself.

Dear single self,

Set aside thirty days. I have found in my own life, when I commit to doing something for thirty consecutive days, change happens. A new habit is formed by repetition and it is consolidated often with a month's worth of doing something every day.

Read a chapter of this book each day, which consists of a short encouragement from me, letters written by women of all ages to their former single selves and a Yestember dare. These dares have been designed to help you to do something small, a task to take you out of your comfort zone and create opportunities for new things.
Adventures? Friendships? Possibilities?

Say yes, to any unique and random opportunities that come your way this month. I found that the older I got, the less likely I was to say yes to opportunities to meet new people. Say no to another work assignment, no to another "have to" for your family. Start saying yes to yourself, saying yes to those opportunities that you have never taken before and those very things that put you in an uncomfortable zone. This book is not about grabbing your quilt and finding comfort; it is about change. Let go of the need to please people and try to delve deep into that which you have been ignoring in your own life.

Don't overcomplicate this either. If you need to read a chapter the night before and do the Yestember dare the day after, then let it flow. If you miss a day, just keep going, don't give up!

Are you ready?

"Make a radical change in your lifestyle and begin to boldly do things which you may previously never have thought of doing, or been too hesitant to attempt. So many people live within unhappy circumstances and yet will not take the initiative to change their situation because they are conditioned to a life of security, conformity, and conservation, all of which may appear to give one peace of mind, but in reality nothing is more damaging to the adventurous spirit within a man than a secure future. The very basic core of a man's living spirit is his passion for adventure. The joy of life comes from our encounters with new experiences, and hence there is no greater joy than to have an endlessly changing horizon, for each day to have a new and different sun. If you want to get more out of life, you must lose your inclination for monotonous security and adopt a helter-skelter style of life that will at first appear to you to be crazy. But once you become accustomed to such a life you will see its full meaning and its incredible beauty."

Jon Krakauer, Into the Wild

CHAPTER THREE

Say Yes!

Can you remember the first time you realised, that maybe you weren't that good at something?

I think the older we get, the more tentative we become, aware of our failures, aware of our imperfections and moments where we just get stuck. Our relationships are the first to be affected when we are worried about what other people think.

Very quickly, we start to question and doubt our abilities.

We start to shut down. Without even realising it, we have backed ourselves into a corner and played the movie forward and so often we just end up saying no.

As children, we change from these young girls, who dance freely around the kitchen whenever music is played, to women who are uncomfortable that we may look silly or childish or, even worse, fat.

As young girls, we play up to the camera, wanting someone, anyone to take our photo. We smile and we play, then one day we become shy and worried about whether we are good looking enough? Is what we are wearing okay? What others will think of us?

As young women, we cook with delight, making the most awful breakfasts for our Mums in bed, with burnt toast and cold coffee, all the while being so proud. As we grow older we become afraid of inviting guests over for dinner, because our food isn't up to a master-chef standard.

We draw and scribble outside of the lines as a toddler and preschooler. Then we hear negative words, one after another; that we shouldn't paint the sky purple, that girls must like butterflies and boys trucks, and our self worth, year after year, becomes squashed into a place of perfection.

The little girl who decorates her room with scarves and colours, dressing up her Barbie dolls with bright colours, building teepees and forts out of rugs... becomes afraid to invite anyone over to her house because it might not look like those amazing homes on Instagram or Pinterest.

We start to say no to new opportunities out of fear and we progressively shut down our lives until we're in a place of comfort. I believe there are times in our life that we just need to make a crazy change and begin to do things that we have never done before. Old ways won't open new doors. Sometimes you just need to throw caution to the wind and say yes.

That's what this book is designed to provoke by using the thread called Yestember: saying yes to things we would not normally do.

Stretching our comfort zones, meeting new people.

Seeing your life with new eyes.

> *"For I am about to do something new. See, I have already begun! Do you not see it? I will make a pathway through the wilderness. I will create rivers in the dry wasteland."*
>
> *Isaiah 43: 19*

Yestember began for me when one of my friends was having a really hard time in the whole realm of singleness.

I realised that she had shut down many opportunities to do new things. She had an amazing business, she was approachable, competent and emotionally stable.

In fact, she was totally brilliant. Despite all these fantastic things, she had stopped doing new things. Thirty-something and still single, she was desperate for change. I had a little idea. I wrote 30 things for her to do in the month of September and she did it.

Day after day, rather than ruminating about her relationship status on Facebook, she put her thoughts and spare time into completing these tasks. She started saying yes and new opportunities came her way. She entertained friends more often, went out more frequently and generally just became happier.

And guess what?

On October 1st, no exaggeration, she randomly met someone and the rest is history.

Ok, major disclaimer; the 30 adventures she went on did not miraculously bring a guy into her life. It was the change in her whole demeanour and her new attitude of throwing caution to the wind and just letting the whole intensity of the single walk slide away.

She was open to random encounters with strangers, she let some walls tumble down, she was full of confidence after a month full of adventures and creativity.

So, here is your first Yestember opportunity.

1. SAY YES TO THIS PROJECT.

I mean really say yes. Not a half-hearted I'm going to try or maybe we will see if this works.

I mean a real yes, boots and all! I'm telling my friends, I'm posting about it on social media... Like really, every day I am going to seize the little opportunity and I am going to plan the parties and the barbecues and step out of my comfort zone.

Saying yes means finding someone who makes you accountable too. Phoning a friend right now and saying "I am committing to reading this book each day and doing these random little acts of kindness for myself. Will you hold me accountable?"

Take a little photo of yourself and put it as your screen saver on your mobile to remind you. Maybe write a status on Facebook declaring the challenge you have set yourself to say yes more often.

When someone asks you out on a date, even though they are 'not really your type', just say yes.

Say yes and take time each day to reflect on where you are at and make a plan for tomorrow.

"Sometimes what we learn and who we become in the process of waiting is even more important than what we're waiting for."

Mandy Hale

Dear single self,

You are a child of wonder and untapped creativity, adventure and strength. Do not be in such a hurry to grow up and become someone's wife. Find out who you are, explore the world, explore people, taste from a wide range of cups. Travel; please get on a plane and go somewhere!

Let go; stop trying to control every aspect of your life and just let some things happen and go with it. Stop trying to always do the right thing. Sometimes there is no such thing as the right thing, the right time or Mr Right. There could be a Mr Right Now; who you will miss because you are so busy looking for Mr Right. Find out about you; there is so much to you. You don't need another half, you are whole on your own. Learn a language, read books, take cooking classes.

Learn to paint; spend more time at the ocean, it feeds your soul. Spend money on shoes. Enjoy all the experiences presented to you without worrying about the future.

Enjoy yourself with a variety of people. They will bring out different things in you, many of which you may not have known you had. Find out who makes you excited, who makes you laugh, who makes you think, who makes you feel beautiful.

Let yourself be loved by others, and love others. Maybe have your heart broken and rebuilt. It will give you strength. Cherish yourself. Love yourself, enjoy you. Feel whole, feel complete. Life does not begin when you are married. Life is now. Enjoy every minute.

Being married is only one path in life and to take that path you give up many others. Once you are married and then perhaps a mother, you limit many things and experiences. You love being both, but your world reduces, so enjoy the wide open spaces of being single. Live life to the fullest, capture each day and find out what an amazing, beautiful, strong, creative and intelligent woman you are.

Realise that the man you marry is very, very lucky to have you.

I love you.

(I was married just three months after my 21st birthday to a man I knew for less than a year. I was raised on the idea of Mr Right and that I would start living when I found that man. I am still happily married, 18 years later)

CHAPTER FOUR

Over Thinker

Waking up the morning after we have done something for the first time, is always a shock to the system. You know that sinking feeling of regret, the moment you have done something risky.

It might not be the morning after for you, it might be the afternoon coffee break or it might be as you drive home contemplating the last twenty-four hours.

No matter when, we all have moments of regret.

Why did I do that?

Why did I say that?

Why did I send that text to that guy?

Why, why, why...

We are a generation of over thinkers, worrying about everything we have said, done and then not done. Some days we just need to stop over thinking and just let go.

You cannot change what has already gone in the past. All you can do is live in this present moment, learning lessons from the past but not setting up camp, with a tent and kitchen sink.

Are you stuck in the past?

Are you stuck in a failed relationship, wondering what you did wrong?

Today is the day to take steps towards letting go.

Letting go is a very private and personal ritual. What is coming to mind as you read this chapter? What do you need to let go of?

Maybe throwing away some letters, maybe journalling a stream of thoughts giving yourself permission to move on, maybe sharing a story with a friend and asking her to pray for release of the burden.

I am making a commitment with you today, to stop over thinking and allowing myself to move forward with purpose and potential.

How about you?

"For what it's worth: it's never too late or, in my case, too early to be whoever you want to be. There's no time limit, stop whenever you want. You can change or stay the same, there are no rules to this thing. We can make the best or the worst of it. I hope you make the best of it. And I hope you see things that startle you. I hope you feel things you never felt before. I hope you meet people with a different point of view. I hope you live a life you're proud of. If you find that you're not, I hope you have the courage to start all over again."

F. Scott Fitzgerald

2. BUY A COFFEE FOR A STRANGER.

Today's adventure will be easy for some and completely terrifying for others. I am asking you to go and buy a coffee for a stranger.

As you walk past your cafe of choice, buy a drink for yourself and then one for another. Whether you pay for the next person in line, or you buy a takeaway and give it to someone as you walk back to your car, it's your choice.

You need to step out of your comfort zone today and do something for someone; someone who can never repay you.

If you are that way inclined, say a little prayer and ask for direction. Then do it.

The most important part of today's adventure is to not over think it. Seriously, just jump in and have a go.

I am sure a smile will surface at some point in your day as you reflect on the moment you shared with a stranger.

And yes, they need to be a complete stranger!

"Look at you. You're young. And you're scared. Why are you so scared? Stop being paralysed. Stop swallowing your words. Stop caring what other people think. Wear what you want. Say what you want. Listen to the music you want to listen to. Play it loud as you want and dance to it. Go out for a drive at midnight and forget that you have school the next day. Stop waiting for Friday. Live now. Do it now. Take risks. Tell secrets. This life is yours. When are you going to realise that you can do whatever you want?"

Louise Flory

Dear Single Self,

Honey stop!

Stop thinking you're not good enough.

You're beautiful and have so much life inside you. Don't be afraid to live it.

Don't look for a guy to fill that void.

For a start, you deserve so much better and secondly you need to grow up a bit more.

Find something you love and take a risk doing it afraid.

Don't follow someone else's passion. It'll just leave you empty.

When you find your passion then you will be so fulfilled, you will be ready for the guy that is meant to fully complement you.

Slow down and wait for real love.

PS – By the way, kids are gold. Love each day with them and stress less.

PPS – You'll do amazing

Love,

Me

(I am now 41 and I got married when I was 20 and had to get my father's permission to marry...)

CHAPTER FIVE

Exhausted

I only realised how exhausted I actually was that summer when I stopped – just stopped filling my life with people, projects, stress, moments...

Not giving time to myself to regroup and recover. Anything that would stop me from being by myself, where my thoughts would surface.

Where is your energy meter sitting right now?

Do you feel alive, fresh and adventurous? Or drained, peaked, stressed and overwhelmed?

I found in the midst of my single wallowing, I had collected a lot of internal and external baggage along the way. I felt cloudy, unclear and cluttered.

Exhaustion has the capacity to do this to us. We end up leaving parts of our lives to grow and fester as we try to keep up with our daily demands.

How is the internal and external clutter in your life?

Is it time to throw away some stuff and create more space in your life for the new.

As we say yes to new opportunities we need to say goodbye to the old, to make space.

There is only so much we can carry with us into new seasons, both internally and externally.

A scripture I love is this one...

> *"Are you tired? Worn out? Come to me. Get away with me and you'll*

recover your life. I'll show you how to take a real rest. Walk with me and work with me; watch how I do it. Learn the unforced rhythms of grace. I won't lay anything heavy or ill-fitting on you. Keep company with me and you'll learn to live freely and lightly."

Matthew 11: 28 – 30

I love the line "Learn the unforced rhythms of grace." How easy is it to force our lives and hearts into a place of should's, rather than just allowing moments from the past to remain there and let go of the burdens that make our hearts heavy.

I always feel light and free when I take time to declutter, letting go of baggage that has been hindering me.

One of the worst feelings is when I have travelled a long distance carrying clothes and luggage that I just didn't need for the destination.

I would fill up my suitcase, stressing that I just might not have enough and then I drag this weight around airports and taxis, despising that I haven't learnt to travel lightly yet again.

Our daily lives are exactly the same. Now is the time to reflect on what is in your life, and consider what is not necessary anymore.

Is it a cupboard full of clothes that needs culling?

Is it a pile of letters from an ex, that need to be burnt?

Is it a cupboard full of long unused clutter?

Is it some behaviours, addictions and quiet weaknesses that no-one knows about?

This is the time of the journey when we have the opportunity to let go of some of the burdens for good.

It is time to internally and externally declutter. Exhaustion is often coupled with baggage. Want to let go of some stuff?

Let's go.

3. DECLUTTER.

Whether it is midnight or 6 o'clock in the morning before work, the time has come to throw out some stuff.

Our external worlds often mirror our internal dispositions.

When we hold onto stuff in our everyday environments, we tell ourselves subliminally that we are not worthy of a clean space and a great home space to thrive in.

What does your bedroom look like?

Are there piles of clothes that you can never get through?

Or is it the opposite?

Is it completely boring, plain and sterile?

Today is the day to start the transformation of your everyday space and to start throwing away, creating space for beauty, peace and reflection.

"Modern life is becoming so full that we need our own ways of going to the desert to be relieved of our plenty."

Thomas Moore

Dear single self,

I am now 45 years old. I got married two years ago when I was 43. Late, some would say!

I now have the most precious seven-month-old baby girl and God has blessed me unreservedly. My husband is a wonderful, kind man.

My life has changed completely. So I am writing back to myself aged 25 ...

Let go of the angst of getting older without being in a relationship. Remember and believe that you are a valuable, loved and loveable human being.

Don't hang on to poor relationships; if someone does not love and value you, they are not going to change. This is not good enough for you and it is far better to be single than to be in a damaging relationship. I have friends who are single and married, even divorced. They are all valuable and loved. God loves each of them and their lives have worth and value apart from marriage.

Saying this, however, it is important to be proactive; don't be a shrinking violet. Believe in yourself. You know that you want to get married and have children some day and you will make a wonderful wife and mother.

You are a strong person and you need to be confident to be yourself and not try to please others all the time. Try not to feel shy and that others may not like you; it is not true. Always make an effort with others. Be a good friend; you have many. Value them and they will value you.

Have a range of interests and make sure you always make that effort to go out and meet new people when you have the opportunity.

God has a plan for you; a good plan filled with hope. He has given you many gifts. Stop thinking about yourself and focus on using them and not wasting precious years.

Yours forever,

Me

CHAPTER SIX

Who are You?

I dated a guy in my late teens and early twenties, who really changed my perspective on guys and physical attraction.

He was a drummer. A popular guy about and around town. You know the type, the one who all the girls fawned over (or I thought so anyway).

I was always overwhelmed that he had chosen me. His popularity bought with it great insecurity in my heart about whether I could sustain his love and affection.

I remember nights being so worried about what I was going to wear, moments at gigs when he was up on the stage, being so overwhelmed at my appearance and whether people thought I was good enough to be dating the drummer.

I remember the night that he rang me from Broome, Western Australia, where he was playing a huge gig, to tell me that he had been with another girl.

My heart broke and I tried to fix its shattered pieces by rebuilding my life around a new premise, believing that all a guy was looking for was a perfect, skinny and pretty girl.

One that I could never be. I had already struggled through my late years of high school with a overwhelming eating disorder, completely convinced that no-one could love me if I was bigger than the models on television.

This new level of brokenness, after my long term boyfriend cheated on me, brought out a whole new level of dysfunction in my body image and how I responded to any guy who was pursuing me. I struggled for years to truly find out who I was.

I grappled. I wrestled. I hated on myself. I despised who I was. I dug a hole so deep I am amazed that I found my way out of it. I wrestled the misconception for decades that no-one would love me unless I was prettier and externally perfect.

Enter a very buff, kind and caring body builder many years later and, year by year, anniversary by anniversary, pregnancy after pregnancy, he is proving that my misconceived notions of beauty were completely unfounded.

I had a long, slow road of recovery to walk down before I could accept my husband's love but mostly I had to come to a place where I truly became steady and grounded in who I actually was.

Internally

Externally

Spiritually

The whole box and dice.

I needed a self worth makeover. I needed to discover who I truly was before I could offer that to someone else to love as well.

How are you going in the area of self worth and esteem?

Can you clearly explain and feel comfortable with who you are?

One of my greatest endeavours, was to find out where I fitted in the bigger purpose. Then and only then did I find my sense of worth with perspective. It was through a deep exploration of being the beloved of an amazing Creator God that changed me irrevocably. Discovering who I was in the light of his plans for my life made the most astounding changes.

Discovery is never an easy pursuit but the end result is ever impacting.

What parts of your life have you believed lies?

Is this holding you back from trusting or allowing another person to see who your truly are?

"Do your thing. Do it every day. Do it 'unapologetically.' Don't be discouraged by criticism. You probably already know what they're going to say. Pay no mind to the fear of failure. It's far more valuable than success. Take ownership, take chances and have fun. And no matter what, don't ever stop doing your thing."

Asher Roth

4. WRITE A LETTER TO YOURSELF.

It is time for you to write a letter to yourself.

There are many letters that have been penned by my friends to their former single self. It is now your turn. Get out a nice piece of paper. Light a candle. Grab a cup of tea or coffee. Take a deep breath and just start to write.

What is it that you have truly believed about yourself in this journey?

What is it that you need to rediscover again?

Who has influenced you either negatively or positively?

Or ignore all of these questions and just write.

Give someone the letter in an envelope with a stamp on it and ask them to post it to you, whenever they believe the time feels right.

"Loving yourself invites others to love you. Respecting yourself invites people to respect you. It all starts with you."

Mandy Hale

Dear single self,

Breathe; I want to tell you a few things that may change your outlook on your future.

First things first, have a bit of cake. It won't kill you, nor will it make you obese. Obsessing over your image for the next few years will only harm you and your future relationships.

You don't need to be skinny to be accepted, or to fall in love. What you are doing to yourself will only serve to make you both physically and mentally exhausted, and the man you meet and marry will love you regardless of what dress size you are.

Yes, I know, right now things are pretty hectic. You have a social calendar to balance, and nothing could be more important, right? Wrong.

What are important right now are the few quality friends you have made who will stick by you over the next couple of years. You will travel with these girls, make lifelong memories, be completely unravelled by them and totally supported through the process. On your wedding day, a few years from now, you will have them stand beside you as your bridesmaids.

When you have your first child, they will be there to support you too.

I know what you really care about right now is finding your future husband, and let me reassure you, he is more wonderful and better looking than you have ever dreamt of. You will meet him right when you least expect it in 2009, and in 2012 you will get married, followed by having a baby a couple of years after that.

Yes, that's right, all your prayers and dreams come to fruition. It won't always be easy, and neither should it be; all great things take love and effort.

So just breathe. Stop trying to wish life by, and take in the little moments that surround you. Some day you will treasure these memories and remember (most of) them fondly.

And some day really soon you will be sitting right where I am sitting at this very moment, having just kissed your stud of a husband goodnight, and rubbing your full term pregnant belly waiting for your first child to enter the world.

Love, C.

CHAPTER SEVEN

Ritual

If you are anything like me, you have got to this part of the book and maybe you are thinking it's just too hard.

You know those books that sit on your beside table, the ones in your kindle that stay on the same bookmark for two years.

Life takes over.

Work happens.

Dramas ensue.

We forget what we were trying to do for ourselves and we forget the resolution of change.

Life moves on.

"Lose the all-or-nothing mentality that resolutions engender; instead practise daily rituals that slowly take root over time."

Mary Carlomagno

Whether we are single, married, divorced or not interested, it is important as women that we take time to bring special rituals into our everyday lives to bring perspective and little shifts of change.

The diets never work, the personality make-overs never last, because we so often want quick, fast consumerist-style fads to bring change to our lives.

If it has taken us twenty years to arrive at our current destination, we are not going to be able to change the location overnight. We have hidden flaws, unrealistic expectations and moments of complete naivety as to why we are in the place that we are in.

I am a strong believer in ritual. Moments when I pause and reflect, writing in my journal about what I am learning, what is frustrating me, and what is overwhelming me.

A candle being lit as the sun goes down reminds me that another day has finished and a time of peace and reflection now surrounds my home.

A glass of wine whilst making dinner, allowing myself to relax and enjoy slowing down.

A walk in the morning to greet the new day and say goodbye to the last.

Do you have any rituals in your life that allow you to reflect and transition well between the seasons?

Do you have times when you are able to reflect and allow yourself to breathe in the midst of the expectations in your world?

Is it a coffee with a friend every Monday evening?

Is it a date with a television series each week and a friend who comes and accompanies you with your television friends?

Is it a special meal that is cooked each Sunday night and you invite friends over?

A secret coffee club?

A divine sisterhood meeting?

We all need little markers of ritual and celebration in our weeks, but even more so those who return to a bed alone each evening.

Creating rituals amongst the every day ordinary makes your life divine.

This book is not about a 30-day plan to get hitched, it is all about changing your mindset in your everyday and creating the life that you desire to live.

"She designed a life she loved."

The only person designing your life is you. You choose what you do with your days. You choose how you spend your evenings. You are your life's designer partnering with a greater being.

Make ritual a part of its light and shade. Make rituals that make you feel happy and connected to a world outside of social media and technology.

5. COOK A RECIPE YOU HAVE NEVER COOKED BEFORE!

Sometimes we just need to do something we have never done before. For no particular reason, but to just enjoy the process.

Start a new ritual: maybe fill your weekend with something homey, invite over someone new to taste it with you.

One of my favourite scenes from a movie is in 'Bridget Jones's Diary' when she cooks the blue string soup.

She had all these grand plans, but her delightful dinner besties ate the blue soup with glee and pronounced her culinary expertise.

New memories can only be made when we do something we have never done before.

So have a go.

Bake some bread.

Make a Moroccan feast.

Start a dinner club with a few other singles in your local community.

Do something daring!

"This is my invariable advice to people: Learn how to cook – try new recipes, learn from your mistakes, be fearless, and above all have fun!"

Julia Child, My Life in France

Dear single self,

Well to start, you weren't single for long before you settled down and married by 23. Having had a baby at 22, the road you found yourself on was very different to those of your young and single friends. I think the biggest thing I would say to you would be that you worried too much about who would love you, that this led to making decisions that set your course on a more difficult path than it should've been.

The short years of your single-ness were a little too consumed with squandering finances on reckless moments. Would've been great if you poured that cash into travelling and acquiring more experiences overseas while you had no responsibility. Getting a credit card at 19 was not the smartest thing you've ever done either. Also, I think your shy demeanour let others walk over you a few too many times.

So be more sure of yourself.

Don't question yourself just because someone else's opinion is louder.

Speak up.

Speak out.

Try harder. Fail more.

Be less lukewarm – in everything you say yes to.

Be less nonchalant.

Wake up earlier and make the most out of your day.

Believe in your talent.

Live bigger than your own self.

But live today to the fullest. Tomorrow will worry about itself. You don't have to have a clear picture of your entire life right now. Just take one step ahead of another and trust in God's provision.

Lastly, you definitely should've loved your body more. It was bangin'. With and without the post-baby stretch marks. If anything, it has helped me to appreciate the strength I have now before the ageing process seeps into these bones and take over completely.

Oh and thanks. Thanks for the hard yards that have led you here, to a place of peace ... freedom ... contentment ... and a hope for what's still ahead.

Always,

34-year-old me.

CHAPTER EIGHT

Hollywood Hysteria

This week marks the end of the latest season of The Bachelor Australia. Oh, the hysteria; the exclusive interview with Woman's Day; the tweets; the 'He said, she said and he did what?'

I sat casually yesterday and had a cup of tea with Mum. She had joined the bandwagon, watched every episode, recorded the finale and bought the t-shirt. Chatting over our tea, we discussed who won, who lost, what words were said and the fact they had broken up only six weeks after the massive ring was proposed with.

Hollywood creates a hype and hysteria that surrounds popular culture in the belief that romance can only be found on an African safari, with candles, luxury and lavish proposals.

Our brains are conditioned with expectations that are unreal and the dating landscape has been pumped full of steroids, with men unsure of how to compete with the image that is projected from our small screens.

I remember watching Jerry McGuire as a competent and handsome Tom Cruise smoothly declared his love for a single mum, with the words "You complete me."

My heart leapt, my expectations rose and I waited for that day when my husband would complete me. I held onto that expectation year after year, and anyone would have thought that my relationship was going to come served with a side of popcorn and ice cream.

It doesn't matter how much we know that the notion of romance from

Hollywood is an unattainable dream; we still struggle to comfortably find love in our everyday.

We are stuck between the image and the reality. We struggle to authentically be okay with normal. We all want the prince to come in on the white horse and rescue the princess who is enslaved by the horrible stepmother.

We are conditioned from a very young age to believe that this is the only way love can be found.

Enter reality.

Eating a Vegemite sandwich while sitting on a beach full of seaweed.

A husband who forgets it's Mother's Day and buys a block of chocolate from the local deli on his way home from work.

The early days of marriage when the presents are starting to break, the dishes piling up and the washing mounts in the laundry.

Hollywood is a liar and we have taken its bait hook, line and sinker.

It is intentionally designed to create hype and social media has exacerbated its need to compete and compare with one another.

The engagement proposals are getting wilder and wilder, the wedding photographers more expensive and intrusive, and honeymoons so extravagant in the hope that we will make a matrimonial splash no-one will ever forget, all the while stealing our mortgage deposits.

Something has to change. We need to put more work into the day after the wedding than the day of the wedding.

We need to allow our potential beaus to romance us with a peanut butter sandwich on a park bench rather than a radical production effort of a date to sweep us off our feet in reality television style.

What if a guy was making small advances towards you in the coffee shop, but they were simply coated in a shy smile and an extra effort in a hello?

What if men were too afraid to ask us out on a date, because our expectations created by 'The Bachelor' can never be met?

What if we have stopped a love affair from blossoming because "He just isn't buff enough."

We have become very shallow and our expectations are robbing us from the beauty that is found in simplicity.

Yet we have the audacity to cry "There are just no guys out there!"

A simple life lived with realistic expectations, and hard working people loving their kind of normal; this is a pursuit of beauty. Everyday. Loving life. Doing ordinary well.

Now that's a storyline Hollywood would reject, but that is a life worth pursing.

"dear future husband,

On road trips, I plan on eating donuts and sleeping in the passenger's seat.

I hope you're okay with the whole driving part.

love, your future wife."

6. ARRANGE DINNER IN THE CITY WITH A GROUP OF PEOPLE.

I know I kind of believed that my husband would knock on my front door someday, or I would have this crazy story where we both meet randomly and he would be instantly amazed by me.

The reality is, we just used to hang out with each other, in a group with many different people. After church, we would go to a restaurant and we would eat. We would chat. We slowly got to know each other, with no expectation from either side that we would eventually become an item.

How often do you hang out with groups of people?

How often do you meet new people?

Do you go to work, come home, hang out with the same people every day, each weekend?

Old ways won't open new doors!

You need to step out and create opportunities to meet new people. Organise a dinner and get everyone to bring a plus-one, somebody who is not already taken. Organise a barbecue for no reason other than just to hang out with people.

That is your task for today; create opportunities to meet new people.

Dear single self,

You are beautiful. You are whole. You are strong.

You don't need to prove anything to anyone, you only need to stand right with your Saviour. You're not missing out, you're walking in God's perfect timing.

I know you have questions, I know you feel like you're missing out.

I know you blame yourself for being too fat, too loud, too picky.

I know you've tried everything; you've tried the miracle diets, the new clothes, the new hair style and even that new lipstick but you're still spending those Saturday nights alone ...

Ah my friend you are in your perfect season. Savour your single moments.

Block out those lies that have been confessed over you, fight the constant need to compare, lose your obsession with your appearance and enjoy life.

Your rainbow may be around the corner but right with you everyday are opportunities that you slip past: take every one.

You will get married. You will find your slice of perfection. You will see your dreams fulfilled, you just need to believe.

Love,

Me

Ps: I have been married for three years now with two babies; two years old and eight months. I was 29 when I got married and I'm 31 now.

CHAPTER NINE

Embrace Rest

It is so difficult to just say we are doing nothing.

"What are you doing this weekend?" "Oh nothing..." Enter the awkward silence.

"What are you doing tonight?" "Oh, a night of rest by myself." Enter questions like, "Are you okay?" "Is everything alright?"

We feel like our Instagram feed is a measure of our success and if it is not full of interesting feats and amazing locations then we are boring.

Our culture does not empower the sacredness of space. Our culture does not promote wellness and the Sabbath. Our culture does not teach us to simply breathe and relax.

We need to embrace rest in a culture of busy. When I went on this journey of discovery in learning to love myself, I was awful at resting.

I was like an obnoxious toddler, screaming at the idea of a midday nap. I stomped my feet, banged on the door and declared that I would not sleep, no matter how tired I felt.

It was when I stopped, it was when I was alone, that the true tone of my inner world became exposed. If I could just escape myself then maybe everything would be okay.

There are many studies that confirm we are addicted to caffeine, we are obsessed with being the best, having the best and living in the biggest house attainable.

We don't want to be left behind and the thought of being alone with our own restfulness is overwhelmingly scary.

I remember being out to dinner by myself in the city and a lovely but nosey waiter said to me, “Miss, are you travelling from interstate?” I said to him “No, why?”

He said, “I just don’t understand why someone like you would be having dinner by themselves.”

I honestly hated that conversation. I did not want to be having dinner alone again.

I had come to the place where cooking for one was such an effort, that dining alone at least in a place where other people were present made me feel less vulnerable and lonely.

He had stated the obvious. He had highlighted my weakness.

Now remembering that night and that conversation, I smile as I was on a journey of discovery about being okay with me. I had many friends that I could have had dinner with that night.

I had a massive family, just a short drive away, but I needed to discover who I was with no other company.

I had to learn to be okay with my own thoughts.

There are many married people who never learn to be okay on their own and consequently they become their own biggest enemy.

I learnt many important lessons in my years of solo dining, and they hold me in a strong place of comfort on the nights now when I am alone with my two small children in a beach shack whilst my husband is on night shift.

It cracks me up, but the one thing I now long for is time alone.

If I get to go to the local shops by myself it is like winning the lottery: space, my own thoughts. The thing I loathed is now the very thing I long for.

Learning to rest in a culture of busy.

As a single person, learning to self-care and not give every part of ourselves to someone, so that you can have company with anyone. Learning to be okay with our own company is a gift that will hold us secure for the rest of our lives.

7. GO SPEND TIME ALONE, SOMEWHERE IN NATURE.

George Santayana said, "The earth has music for those who listen."

If you struggle to find time to be alone, maybe you struggle with the whole notion of your thoughts and the way being by yourself makes you feel.

Maybe you don't, maybe you are just busy.

Whether you're just busy or whether you struggle with the thoughts that arise as you sit in a space of silence and aloneness, we all need to settle in a space where we are okay with just being.

The habit of contemplation, the habit of simply being, is not an easy skill for our tech obsessed and over stimulated senses.

I live less than twenty paces from the ocean, yet I struggle to walk out into nature and allow my thoughts and life to breathe.

Will you commit with me, to finding an hour and going into a space of nature and allowing the thoughts to just come?

To soak up the view, to bathe in the beauty of nature and make a habit to just be.

To rest.

To love your messiness.

To be.

Dear single self,

I am now 32 and got married when I was 21! Really, are you ready for this? Will you ever be?

You know the season will come (eventually), but that's not really the point. Wedding season is full of excitement, but it leads to married season and kids season and work season and tired season and getting grey hair season and, well, you get the point.

We were speaking the other night about being 'prepared'.

My usual theory is that you will never be completely ready for the next season of your life, so just get on with it. The Bible has a lot to say about seasons; that they will always exist and that preparing for the one coming up is a pretty good idea.

Before you have children, people say, "It'll change your whole life" but I beg to differ.

Here are some things it didn't change: who I was married to, the house I lived in, where I worked, my extended family, my church, my dog, the food I liked, the interests I had, my eye colour, etc, etc. It definitely changed many of my relationships, the time and finance I had at my disposal and my character. But, it didn't change my whole life!

Sometimes, we think that the next season of our life means everything is going to change, and when it doesn't, we're disappointed! Your whole life doesn't change when you get married, only some of it does. If you hate your job, getting married won't help. If you are stuck in a food rut, don't change your relationships, change what you eat.

Before you get married, people say lots of (strange, unusual and sometimes unhelpful) things. You really should ignore most of them (except when it's your Mum; she does know everything). How you feel about yourself won't change. If you wanna hide from things now, it gets harder when you live with someone you hopefully wanna impress.

Getting married at 21 was not in my 'original' plan.

But I am better for it. We are both better for it. The age is actually not the important part, the surrender is the important part. The selflessness that is learnt is the hardest and importantest (I know that's not a word!) part.

Being realistically prepared for the change that the next season will (and won't) bring is a healthy way to live. It helps you to be emotionally and mentally balanced. God never reveals to us the whole plan in full detail, but He does use our current experience to prepare us for what's ahead. We just need to take notice.

Love,

Me

"Four things on earth are small,
yet they are extremely wise:
Ants are creatures of little strength,
yet they store up their food in the summer"

Proverbs 30:24 – 25

CHAPTER TEN

Hope deferred

I was single for all my twenties and most of my thirties. I was Katherine Hiegel from "27 Dresses". Always the bridesmaid, never the bride.

I even got to the place where I had decided 'That is it, I am not going to be a bridesmaid any more.' It didn't matter who offered me the privilege of being part of their special day. My heart and my bank account could not handle one more ugly dress.

The honest truth, though, wasn't that I didn't enjoy being part of my friends' special events; the plain truth was that my heart was very sick.

There is a proverb that puts it perfectly.
"Hope deferred makes the heart sick,
but when the desire is fulfilled, it is a tree of life."

Proverbs 13:12

If there was a doctor who dealt with hearts – not our blood pumping, life giving one, but our soul, our person, our core. I needed one.

Bitterness,

Doubt,

Disappointment,

Offence.

They had all taken residence in my internal house and I did not know how to kick them out. Having your hope deferred is a difficult place to find yourself in.

Often you are in that place, because you cannot find anyway to fulfil the desire, dream or longing in your own power. You have to wait, you have to rely on others and, for me, I had to trust something bigger and more powerful than myself.

God.

I wanted to find a husband who was a great leader, a man of faith, someone who would be able to stand alongside me in the dreams and desires I had for my life.

To find that kind of person, I needed to continue to grow in myself but also continue to trust that God had greater plans and ways than I could ever see or know.

His ways were higher than mine. His plans were greater than mine.

And in that place of deferral, I had to find a way to let go of my disappointment, my anger, my bitterness and my layer upon layer of offence.

I had to let go of the potential that the desire might not come together in the way that I planned and trust that in the end I wanted to live with a healthy heart not a sick one.

Letting go has never come easy to me. I want to put every effort I have to make my dreams come to pass and sometimes, no matter what we do, time is required for dreams to become a reality.

In the midst of my struggles with hope, I found a poem from the book of Lamentations that helped me find a way to allow my hopes to rise and the sick places of my internal world be flushed out and healed by a God who hears and knows our dreams and desires.

"God proves to be good to the man who passionately waits,
to the woman who diligently seeks.
It's a good thing to quietly hope,
quietly hope for help from God.

It's a good thing when you're young
to stick it out through the hard times.

When life is heavy and hard to take,
go off by yourself. Enter the silence.
Bow in prayer. Don't ask questions:
Wait for hope to appear."

Lamentations 3:25–29

8. TAKE A HEART EXAMINATION?

How is the health of your heart?

Not your physical one, but the heart that represents your soul. Your personhood. Your emotional world. The place where your spirit resides and your mind feeds.

If you could write down one word that describes how you feel in your internal world, what would it be?

Do you feel hopeful?

Do you feel disappointed?

Do you feel overwhelmed?

One of the best ways to help hope arise again is to take time to write a stocktake of how you are really feeling.

To write until you can't write anymore, to get it out on paper.

Then to take time to release these thoughts and to trust and hope again.

Some people will need help with this process from a friend, a counsellor, a therapist, a pastor.

Others will be okay to take time to pray, to process and to allow hope to rise again.

Today's challenge is to write and allow your true feelings to be expressed and then find someone to process them with to help hope arise.

Dear single self,

I was 28 when I got married after a five-year courtship. I'm 34 now, and we're happier now than we were back then. But not without having travelled some bumpy roads.

I would tell you to Live. REALLY live.

Be bold. Be adventurous. TRAVEL. Take advantage of the fact that there is nothing tying you down and holding you back. Go and create those stories you will share with your friends. "Remember that time when we..."

Figure out who you are. Take your time, and don't let anyone, and I mean ANYONE, tell you to do something you don't want to.

Don't worry too much about what other people say, and surround yourself with positive, loving people. Know who your real friends are, putting effort into those relationships. Lovers come and lovers go, but your friends, they are the ones who will stay.

While you're at it, remember your family; parents, siblings, cousins, aunts and uncles, they are your rock. Always have been, always will be.

Once in a while; listen to your Mother. And REALLY listen. Believe it or not, sometimes she's right. But also remember, sometimes she's wrong too. Remember she's only human, but she is one of your allies. You will realise at some point she's an amazing lady, and you have worlds to learn from her.

Your heart is a weird, temperamental thing. Your heart is going to flutter when someone interesting glances your way, will pound when they come in for that all important first kiss, and will break when they leave, often without explanations.

It's okay to be heartbroken. It's okay to wallow in your own misery for a little while. Then remember to pick yourself back up. Get out there! When you're willing to take a chance, love will find you (with a little help from on-line dating sites).

I hate to revert to old clichés, but you'll know when the right person has come along. When he does, remember that it's okay to disagree with him, fight with him but also learn from him and listen.

Be true to yourself, and let him be true to himself. That would show you his strength in character; which is so much more important than just good looks.

Laugh together. Talk to together. Listen to each other.

Your life will unfurl before you in ways you can't even begin to imagine. You're going to make mistakes, and so will he. But remember to forgive. And so will he.

You're going to be fine

Love,

You at 34

"Life is unpredictable,
It changes with the seasons,
Even your coldest winter,
Happens for the best of reasons,
And though it feels eternal,
Like all you'll ever do is freeze,
I promise spring is coming,
And with it, brand new leaves."

e.h.

CHAPTER ELEVEN

Growing Up

I have never been someone who struggles with people's ages. If I like someone then I just hang out with them. Some of my best friends are decades older than me and my husband is ten years younger than me. I am okay hanging out with fifty-year-olds and twenty-year-olds, age does not indicate how mature someone is.

It amazes me, when people find out that there is a ten-year age gap between my husband and me, how people react.

It would be completely inappropriate if I was twenty-five when I met him and he was fifteen, but I was thirty-four and he was twenty-four and we hardly ever talked age. Our values were so aligned and never once have I questioned the age difference. In some ways, he is often way more mature than me on many different levels.

We loved each other's company. We had similar passions, similar beliefs, a very focused vision on what we wanted in the future. We were a great match.

I believe the older we get the less age matters and the more maturity becomes important.

You can be fifty and immature or twenty-five and mature. It is all about your character and the way you respond to the everyday ordinary things.

Another problem I have with the age debate is this pressure to be married and have children by the time we are twenty-something.

We don't have to be a certain age to have certain things happen in our lives. We can be so obsessed with an age that we lose sight of the lessons we are learning in that season.

The best spouse is someone who has worked on their character, their integrity, their anger, their kindness... the list goes on.

Never once have I questioned my husband's integrity and never have I seen him respond immaturely in a situation.

He is passionate about growing up and being a man. He is passionate about being a provider and a leader for our family. He is passionate about people and the Creator of humankind.

These are the traits that make him a fabulous father, role model and husband.

Not the age he turns each October on his birthday.

"There is no designated time for anything in your life. You don't have to have your first kiss at any certain time, you don't have to get married in your 20's and you don't have to do anything just because other people think it's best. In fact, you will be much better off if you just do what your heart says. The day you stop caring what other people think is the day their opinions don't mean anything, because you're not there to give them weight." Brianna West

Are you stuck because you have believed a lie that a certain age is required for a certain stage of life?

Have you said no to a friendship with someone because age has become a barrier?

What are your beliefs around this topic?

My personal belief is that maturity is much more important than age when looking for a partner to share life with.

Has the person you are interested in grown up?

Are they a boy or a man?

Can you let them be the man in the relationship or do you always need to have control?

These are questions worthy of being answered whilst in the midst of contemplating relationships over this 30-day journey.

"Love is a temporary madness, it erupts like volcanoes and then subsides. And when it subsides, you have to make a decision. You have to work out whether your roots have so entwined together that it is inconceivable that you should ever part. Because this is what love is. Love is not breathlessness, it is not excitement, it is not the promulgation of promises of eternal passion, it is not the desire to mate every second minute of the day, it is not lying awake at night imagining that he is kissing every cranny of your body. No, don't blush, I am telling you some truths. That is just being 'in love', which any fool can do. Love itself is what is left over when being in love has burned away, and this is both an art and a fortunate accident."

Louis de Berniéres, Captain Corelli's Mandolin

9. HAVE A COFFEE WITH A PENSIONER.

I believe some of the saddest corridors in our communities are the retirement homes in our local area. Lounge rooms where volumes of stories and seasons of wisdom remain untold as senior citizens sit waiting to have tea with some-one, anyone...

Do you know someone in their eighties or nineties?

How long has it been since you sat with them and asked questions about marriage, relationships and growing up?

One of my favourite dating books is by Elisabeth Elliot, 'Passion and Purity'.

She wrote this book in 1984, based on letters she had written to her husband forty years earlier in the 1940's. Years and years of maturity and lessons learnt, holding her in good stead for the advice she was to write. Notice how I am not writing a book about marriage? I have only been married for four short years, but singleness, I was single for about thirty of them and still I have much to learn.

My challenge is to find someone older than eighty and join them in a simple cup of tea while they talk. Let them tell you some stories while you listen.

"If we hold tightly to anything given to us unwilling to allow it to be used as the Giver means it to be used we stunt the growth of the soul. What God gives us is not necessarily 'ours' but only ours to offer back to him, ours to relinquish, ours to lose, ours to let go of, if we want to be our true selves. Many deaths must go into reaching our maturity in Christ, many letting goes."

Elisabeth Elliot

Dear single self,

Don't feel so rushed to grow up.

You are 18, there are so many things to see and do. Take the time.

Be an individual, be proud, be strong.

Enjoy your spare time, don't go looking for company to fill the space. Enjoy the abundance of free time and fill it with things that are meaningful for you.

Love yourself.

Remember this:

Marriage isn't the big fluffy wedding, with 100 guests there to watch you on this one special day. Marriage is the days, weeks, months and years of travelling through the peaks and troughs of life with a person who loves you even when you aren't at your best.

Marriage isn't selfish. It's selfless.

Marriage isn't short. It is a life-long commitment and your 27-year-old self may quit at many things, but she will never quit this one thing. So be sure you are ready to be in for the long haul. Because it will test you.

Marriage isn't individual. It's a team.

And single self, the man we picked; he is a good one. The best. Treat him well. Appreciate him.

Love him.

Love,

Your future self.

"There is something inexpressibly
beautiful about the world
when the sun begins to rise and
fills the dim sky with soft rays of light and
only the birds are awake to sing to you 'good morning',
while everyone else is
curled up in their beds, unaware of the
magnificence they're missing and
everything feels so simple.
It's as if six a.m. is an epiphany
that sparks at your fingertips and
spreads until you are encompassed
entirely by a feeling of clarity.
There is something inexpressibly
beautiful about being awake to behold the
splendour of this world while
everyone else is still asleep."

Madisen Kuhn

CHAPTER TWELVE

Be Mindful

I am listening to the dulcet tones of snoring, watching the light streaming in my window declaring the day has sprung. I love then being able to snuggle back under the quilt. Oh the delight of sleeping in!

Every morning my little man sneaks into my room and yells at the top of his voice, "Wake up, Mummy. Wake up!"

As much as I dislike this early morning human alarm clock, I am learning to love the early morning wakefulness and the sense of inspiration that awaits the dawn.

I remember the feeling of never wanting to get up. I remember being so exhausted and so overwhelmed at the thought of being alone just one more day that all I wanted to do was escape under the blankets.

I remember the early hours of the morning, lying in bed wondering if anyone would ever love me. I remember being awake but feeling like I was sleep-walking because I was so distracted by the thoughts rolling around my head. I was anything but mindful.

Mindfulness is being aware of the moment you are in and engaging in it.

I spent many years trying to escape my present and wanting to go back to bed, hoping no-one would miss me. I spent many hours dreaming about my white wedding, most of which never came to pass.

I was living in the future, wanting to escape the present.

Over that summer of love, I decided to stop waiting for the future to enact my plans. I decided to start really living. To be mindful. To stop the negative thoughts of 'when will I ever...' and to start living, really living in the present.

I had a list of dreams on my bucket list and only one of them was to get married. I sat on my bed one summer evening and I started writing. I wrote all the things I wanted to achieve, I wrote all the places I wanted to travel. I just started writing a list and I finished with 75 things I wanted to do before I went to heaven.

I realised that I had been waiting to have a ring on my finger to start living the life of my dreams.

One of the things on my list was something I had wanted to do since I was fifteen and that was write a book. So I just started.

It was called 'Capture 30 Days of Inspiration' and it was all about living in the moment. Being more mindful about the present and engaging in the inspiration found in my everyday. I did it that January. Every day for thirty days I wrote a chapter and that year I published my first book.

As I started to seek and find inspiration in my everyday, I started to wake with a sense of purpose. Sleeping in was no longer a desire, getting up, finding life and love was my mission. I was living the life I had dreamed of and I didn't have to wait to be married to do so.

I travelled extensively that year, I rode a horse for the first time, I learnt new skills, I booked myself in for an art class...

I became interested in the now and started to forget about the future. I learnt to love myself and respect myself.

I attracted people into my friendship circle who also lived mindfully.

"Your life is shaped by your thoughts"

Proverbs 4: 23

10. WRITE A MESSAGE ON A MIRROR

One of the greatest ways that I engage in my now, is writing scriptures or quotes in places that I can see them everyday.

I have written them on post-it notes and put them on the dashboard of my car. I have a blackboard in my home and I write large messages to myself on it. I have written scriptures on mirrors in my home.

What I am asking you to do is write a message to yourself, somewhere that is very visual. To remind yourself to remain in the moment this month.

Remind yourself that you are Brave, Strong, Courageous, Kind, Beautiful, Worthy of Love.

Whatever words you need to encourage your now, write them in big fat letters and remind yourself that you are loved.

Remind yourself that you are worthy of respect.

Remind yourself of your purpose.

Go do it now.

Go on.

You didn't do it, did you? LOL

Dear single self,

What a journey you have been on. Not one you expected, but one that has shaped you into the beautiful woman you are today.

I bet you never thought you would have reached the place where you are today, how life can slowly piece itself back together and still have good things in your life that bring you love, joy and happiness.

I want to tell you that its okay to cry, to be angry and to grieve. 22 years old is too young to die. But God has it all under his control. 14 years old; now who finds true love so young.

Well you did. Everyone was just waiting until you two got a bit older to become man and wife. But the boy you fell in love with, the boy you thought you would grow old, the boy you shared so many wonderful memories with, suddenly got ill. The word we dread to hear; cancer. Your world shatters at the age of 17. All your hopes and dreams vanish, six months to live. No cure. Time is all you have.

He is a fighter and is granted a few more months here on Earth than expected. Sixteen months after being diagnosed with liver and pancreatic cancer, he meets his Maker.

You walk through dark valleys but I want you to know you will sing from those mountain tops again. Your family loves you and will carry you through those dark days. Your friends will remain by your side. You will put your life back together again. And one day you will find love again.

Surround yourself with people who love God, who will encourage you and pray for you. Make sure you talk to someone you trust about your fears, your hurts and your worries. Don't bottle these up.

You need to learn to love yourself as a single person and love life again. You need to learn to let go, without forgetting. Be brave and start piecing your life back together, only this time the picture will be different.

You are young and you are strong. It will take you some time to mend that heart of yours. One day you will opening that your scarred and fragile heart to someone and they will love you, all of you.

I want you to know that this will happen.

"How long?" you ask; I can't tell you that.

Be assured your love for the one who has passed will not fade, but you will learn to grow more love, so that you can love another as deeply.

You will be alright.

God's got you in His hands.

Trust Him.

Love,

Me

(I gave my life to Christ when I was 14 years old. And only two years later God took me through a dark valley. My faith grew weak while Blair was ill, and once Blair had passed I hated God for what he had done. But God put people in my life to encourage me and carry me through, I learnt that God has a plan and I have to trust him fully. It took me a long time to get to the place where I am now. And though I haven't found that someone to open my heart and fall in love again, I know God listens to my prayers of hopes to marry, to have a family and grow old with someone. It is hard being single as you age. But God has carried me through that very dark valley and I believe he will let me sing for joy one day when I become someone's wife. But in the mean time, I am learning to live and love life as a single woman, and hope I can be an encouragement to others who have / are walking through similar valleys as mine.)

CHAPTER THIRTEEN

The P Word!

There is one word that drove me crazy when I was single. In fact, it still drives me crazy now.

A word so putrid that when it is uttered, people screw their faces up, lift their right eyebrow, look devastatingly into your eyes and say, "What did you just say?"

It was the word that more mature believers would tell me I needed to find. It was the word that was developed when I stood in a line at the shopping centre.

It was the word that was carved deep in my memory as I waited for a photo to upload onto the internet.

The dirty word is only eight letters long, only two syllables deep, yet so infuriatingly confusing.

The P word is ... patience.

Patience?

The most unsuspecting, lovely little old lady, as I tell her my sordid single sorrows, would say to me, "God is just teaching you patience, my dear."

"What did she just say?"

"You told me that I need to be patient?"

"Gah!"

If I am to be completely honest with you, I have nothing to add to the patience debate. I am terrible at it. The only thing that can increase your patience, test your patience and make you patient, is waiting for something.

The question is, how will you wait?

Many years through my single journey, I waited terribly.

I huffed and puffed, I wrestled and wrenched, I controlled and bargained. Then some years, I waited quietly and hopefully with a halo around my head.

Then as quickly as I thought I had earned the patience card, the halo slipped around my neck and I screamed out in anger to God once again.

How does the P word make you feel?

Waiting sucks sometimes, but I know this one thing: it always stretches our capacity and eventually makes us a better person.

Patience is the greatest teacher. It is always drawing us deeper into a place of privilege and presence. Patience makes us breathe. Patience makes us believe in better days.

Patience creates kind humans when it is accepted and surrendered to.

"You must learn to be patient. Patient with yourself and the people in this world. You must learn to slow down. To take some time to breathe, to notice, to appreciate what you have. Just trust that in the moment you really need an answer it will come to you clearly. You will know what you need to do, to say, to give. Believe in yourself, in the life you are leading. Trust that you can and will figure this all out. Give yourself the time and space to do that."

Daniell Koepke

11. JIGSAW PUZZLE TIME.

I have a great friend, her name is Penny. She works so hard and loves crazy deep. Every holiday that she embarks upon with her family, especially at Christmas, she buys one of those massive jigsaw puzzles from a charity shop and places it on the family dinner table.

It is a distinct sign to her family that it is time for them to slow down.

A 5,000 or 10,000 or – dare I say it – 20,000-piece jigsaw puzzle is not for the faint hearted.

It is for the patience warrior who needs to take time to bring it all together.

This is my thought: go and buy a jigsaw puzzle. One of those really big old-style ones and start to piece it together.

It will build patience in you. It will test your patience. It will slow you down.

It will increase your awareness of your thoughts and whether you are in a positive or negative head space.

It will grow you.

Yuck!

Dear single self,

I am now quickly approaching forty and sometimes cannot believe I am where I am. Life has been interesting and challenging at times and there are a few things I wish I could have heard louder.

I believed that I was never good enough for anything or anyone. I struggled with self-image and body image but now I know that is a farce, that believing in myself and knowing I am worth so much more and that God does love me is the most important.

Single self, I thought no-one could love me and sometimes in my early thirties I looked not to God but to other things to give myself a belief that I was worthwhile. I believed that everyone was better at making friends, living life and having a boyfriend.

Then one day in my mid-thirties everything changed. I learnt some lessons that I wish I had learnt earlier. I learnt that life is short so live it; I can only make myself happy; security lies in God even if it doesn't seem so; make the best of what I have; and there is nothing better than living each moment.

Then an amazing thing happened: I met my wonderful husband who is more that I could have ever prayed for or imagined. Even though our four years have had their ups and downs and the mixing of two different cultures has sometimes been interesting, if I had not learnt the lessons I think it would have been harder.

Now I am ever thankful for where I am and thankful for all that I have and thankful that, against all the medical odds, we are expecting our first child and God does fulfil the desires of the heart.

So single self, hold on to your dreams, listen to God and life will turn out better than you could ever imagine.

Love,

Me.

CHAPTER FOURTEEN

A Thunderous Heart

"I own an unsettling, thunderous heart. It beats and melodies. It has turned my life into a play between loving and living." S.L Heart

I have tried four different times to sit and write this chapter but, every single time, distractions have set in.

Even as I write now, I feel uneasy and distracted. It is easy to live our lives this way.

Technology was supposed to make our worlds simpler but, if anything, it leaves us jumping from one thought to the next, finding ways to stay aloof and withdrawn. Lately, I find many distractions prevent me from discovering the deep yearnings of my inner world.

It is not easy to face the real depths of our hearts. Often when we do, we will want to shut down the experience quickly because we do not like the vulnerable feelings that we find exposed there. I have been reading a lot of Breńe Brown over the last year and her teachings have been encouraging me to make peace with the true colour of my soul.

"Owning our story can be hard but not nearly as difficult as spending our lives running from it. Embracing our vulnerabilities is risky but not nearly as dangerous as giving up on love and belonging and joy; the experiences that make us the most vulnerable. Only when we are brave enough to explore the darkness will we discover the infinite power of our light."
Breńe Brown

Are you afraid of the true place your heart sits in today?

Do you tell everyone you are okay when really, if you were completely honest, you would say you feel overwhelmed?

Are you unable to love, because you have allowed fear, disappointment or anger to reside in your heart?

We can so easily dismiss the true conditions of our heart, because it is just too painful to explore the depths. I remember being so afraid of being called 'Emotional' or 'Needy' or, even worse, 'Desperate'.

One thing that has not changed since being married is the way I process seasons and emotions in my world. I still feel. Being married hasn't completed me or made me feel any more significant as a person. In some ways, it has made me question even more than I could ever have imagined, especially since becoming a mother.

What I needed to come to terms with was the person I was, a creative soul, longing to find truth, a deep thinker, a colourful expresser and someone whose heart loved large.

I needed to learn that loving sometimes hurts and you can also be lonely and be married.

I learnt that having a stormy heart wasn't necessarily a bad thing, it was the way I expressed those grey emotions and the way that I drew other people into my vortex that needed to change.

It is okay to feel deeply. Finding ways to walk through those storms and find the sun again, now that is a skill that is nurtured and learnt.

I have a thunderous heart and I'm unapologetic about it. I choose to feel, to love deeply and to express passionately.

I will not sit on the sidelines and commentate about others, I will dive in and learn as I swim, I will encourage extravagantly and think radically. I refuse to be the same person today as I was yesterday.

I will say sorry quickly and do everything in my capacity to let go completely. I get this wrong often, but I am willing to admit that today is a new day and I want to be present in it.

Life is fleeting and I aim to grasp every possible piece of it and revel.

Yes I do indeed own a thunderous heart.

How about you?

12. BOOK A COUNSELLING SESSION.

I believe we all have something deep within us, that hasn't yet been expressed. A secret, some thoughts, some unmet expectations, some desires.

We have seasons when we have let go and other seasons when we feel completely overwhelmed, but I have always found in my walk, there is always something new to learn about ourselves.

There is a simple psychology principle called the Johari window. It is a four-paned piece of glass that sheds light on how we see ourselves and how others see us.

If we were a window, with four panes, we would been seen in four different ways.

1. Things we know about ourselves that nobody else knows (eg secrets).
2. Things we know about ourselves that everyone knows as well (eg I have blue eyes).
3. Things about us that others see but that we have no idea about (eg a fault).
4. Things that we have no idea about and no-one else does either; only God knows (our purpose, potential, future).

I have always found it useful to take time to sit with a professional, whether it be a life coach, a counsellor, a chaplain, a psychologist, a priest, a nun, a pastor, a leader. Maybe sit with an older, mature person. There is wisdom for the older person to teach the younger.

Taking time out to share your heart and ask for reflection.

Why don't you book time to do this sometime this month and simply start to talk about what is being brought up in your internal world.

Dear single self,

Life is worth waiting for!

There is a time for everything in your world. You don't have to rush ahead and make things happen!

How they happen though does depend on your patience and your movement. Don't sit in the boat; get out of it. Can I encourage you now to walk not run. Listen, absorb, breathe...

You have dreams in your heart; they are real. They have purpose and they will come to pass in God's timing.

And God, He is so worth the patience lesson. Things don't hurt in his time and ways.

Stop looking around thinking you know how it will work, it's ok to not know.

Don't assume people's thoughts. Let people speak.

You have time, you are beautiful, growing is good.

Love boldly.

Live unafraid.

Dream big and do!

Your value is far beyond imagination; it is more than you could know, you are amazing to know, to listen to, to love.

Life is good!

Love,

Me

(I got married at 18, had my first baby at 19, got divorced at 23 and remarried at 26. I now have four children and I am 36.)

CHAPTER FIFTEEN

Everyday, Ordinary

Are you disappointed in your everyday, ordinary life?

Ordinary is a pretty boring, average, everyday kind of word. Each one of us has to face the ordinary in our everyday. There are so many ordinary days when they are matched against the extraordinary ones.

Social media has created a pressure and extremism in the way we present our everyday. We need to be multitasking entrepreneurs, with Vogue-worthy living rooms and immaculately presented hair do's, along with being funky, well dressed and make-up ready.

We have these unrealistic expectations of when we should get married, to whom we should get married, with an extravaganza of a wedding day, all documented online.

Popular culture has told us over and over that we are to make our lives count, that we are to do wild and radical things, but what if doing our everyday ordinary lives with Jesus, means to embrace exactly what God is doing in our everyday and that is the main point?

I have realised that, in my singleness, I built up such high expectations of what my husband was going to be, that no-one could ever live up to them.

I remember planning our honeymoon and my fiancé (soon to be husband) said to me, "Amanda, your expectations for this honeymoon are so unrealistic, it wouldn't matter if I took you to the Bahamas, you would still be disappointed."

I had collected lingerie, I had pinned photos in a dream book, I had all these expectations of what my honeymoon would be like but then a few big things shifted in the lead up to our wedding and we decided we would not fly anywhere. We decided that we would drive down south from our new house, we would stay around and hang out with our family who had flown very long distances to be with us at our wedding. We decided to go very low key. Actually very ordinary.

Oh the wasted time dreaming of these far off exotic locations for this holiday of a lifetime.

My honeymoon however, was extraordinary. I loved waking up next to my husband, I loved sleeping with him for the first time, I loved cooking for him, talking about our lives together and just enjoying being together. We were just as excited to go home and set up house, to go to work, to wake up next to each other, to live our lives together.

I remember chatting with someone about her honeymoon and she told me quietly that she cried pretty much every day of their first few weeks together. Expecting it to be so different to what it was, expecting sexy, expecting revolutionary, expecting the dream.

I love this scripture:

> *"So here's what I want you to do, God helping you: Take your everyday, ordinary life – your sleeping, eating, going-to-work, and walking-around life – and place it before God as an offering. Embracing what God does for you is the best thing you can do for him."*
>
> *Romans 12:1*

In a world intoxicated by success and extreme living, everydayness is boring. An Instagram feed that had a bowl of cereal posted everyday would have very few followers.

What if we took our everyday, ordinary lives and looked for the extraordinary moments with Jesus found in the midst of them?

Marriage can be very ordinary. It is easy when we are dating someone to give them the edited and filtered versions of ourselves but everyday, when we have our periods, when we are frustrated, we are angry or disappointed, we can't just check out of a marriage, you need to do the everyday well.

We can dream about what we think doing everyday with someone looks like and create all these unrealistic expectations. We can disengage from reality, looking for perfection, but at the end of the day, we still go to sleep and wake up with sleep in our eyes and often snoring in our ears. We are very human, everyday people, with very normal lives.

Are you looking for a normal, everyday kind of partner to do life with or are you looking for a super hero?

Do you have unreal expectations of what married life is?

Maybe you don't, maybe your expectations are very low, but for those who are stuck in the land of perfection, this chapter is for you...

"He's not perfect. You aren't either, and the two of you will never be perfect. But if he can make you laugh at least once, causes you to think twice and if he admits to being human and making mistakes, hold onto him and give him the most you can. He isn't going to quote poetry, he's not thinking about you every moment, but he will give you part of him that he knows you could break. Don't hurt him, don't change him and don't expect more than he can give. Don't analyse. Smile when he makes you happy, yell when he makes you mad, and miss him when he is not there. Love hard when there is love to be had. Because perfect guys don't exist, but there's always one guy that is perfect for you."

Bob Marley

13. CLEAN SOMEONE'S HOUSE.

Lately I have been learning to let go of my unrealistic expectations of myself and my partner, and to love the very ordinary moments of each day.

One of my favourite books that I have read in the last twelve months was 'One Thousand Gifts' by Ann Voskamp.

She talks about her everyday, ugly moments and finding grace and truth in them. When we sweep the floors, when we wash the dishes, when we serve...

Our everyday, ordinary.

> *"I want to see beauty. In the ugly, in the sink, in the suffering, in the daily, in all the days before I die, the moments before I sleep."*
>
> *Ann Voskamp*

My challenge to you today is to offer to clean someone's house. Or to offer to do something very ordinary, very boring at work and to take your time to discover beauty in its plainness.

Maybe just wash the dishes tonight, and enjoy the simplicity of the moment. The warm water on your hands, the dishes swirling around.

Take time to embrace the ordinary today.

Maybe someone very ordinary is wanting to capture your attention as well.

Dear 16-year-old self,

You are beautiful. When you look in the mirror try to see all the great things instead of comparing your body to a model. You are not fat.

When you think about who you are, try not to dwell on your weaknesses. You can work on them. You can change with perseverance and with the help of your loved ones and God. You can achieve things greater than you can imagine. When people point out your mistakes and weaknesses, try to not take to heart and dwell and wallow on the negatives.

You have some amazing things about you. Try to see the strengths that you have. Ask those close to you what they are. Acknowledge them to yourself and be confident in them. They are God given. You will be able to help others with your compassion, love and encouragement.

When you meet your husband, you will see in him strength of character that you haven't seen in many boys so far. You will imagine that he is too incredible and think that you could never be a partner for him because you have a low opinion of who you are. Listen to your Mum who will encourage you and remind you that you have a wrong judgement of yourself and that you should allow yourself to expect great things for yourself.

Until now, without realising it, romantic stories have been a teacher in your life through fairytales, children's books and movies. Because of this you have a misguided view of love and romance and your expectations of your life partner. This could be a curse on your relationship for many years if you don't realise this soon.

Your expectations for this romance have the potential to blind you to the fundamental strength that is the love that is offered to you by your husband. It is so important that you try to see early on that, while there are five love languages, your husband does not find all of these languages easy to express. His unwavering commitment to you, his integrity and his willingness to be honest and vulnerable are the strengths that he brings to the relationship. Value these things over the 'prince charming' expectations that you have collected without even knowing it.

It seems so simple but it really is true that if you focus on the positives about him you will not have all the stress of having expectations of what you think a fairytale prince should give you. This is the biggest lesson you can learn to be happily married – please try to learn it early.

Remember that your husband has some expectations and needs that you are not fulfilling and that relationship is compromise and it is so important to be thankful for the great things you do have instead of focussing on the things you don't have.

Agree on a budget together and stick to it. Be generous with your time, love and finances to your loved ones and those around you. Don't feel guilty about not being able to give to everything.

Sex is a God-given nurturing part of your relationship. Try to value it, be generous in it and always make an effort to keep it as a positive part of your marriage. Like anything, it continues to get better with practice and commitment.

Have balance in your life. If you work/study all the time, you will become depressed. Make sure you have friendships, fun times and opportunities to be creative. Learn which things help you to feel happy and do some of these things.

Try not to be a worrying mum. I say this knowing it is one of the most difficult things to do. Pray for your children often, do your best to love them and communicate with them. Know that God has given you these children to be their mum so have the confidence that, with His help and the help of others in your life, you can be a good mum. Know that you will fail, but try to acknowledge those failures and apologise to your children and try again. They will have their struggles but they will grow up to be remarkable adults.

Most of all know that your relationship with God is the most important part of your life. Nurture this relationship. Try to read your Bible, pray and go to church and home group often. Read books about faith, grace and bibliographies about how others navigate their walk with God. God will help you in every area of your life if you let Him. Try to acknowledge Him all the time in the good times and bad. Know that He will get you through some of the toughest times in your life and will always have an answer for every problem. Go to those wise men and women you know when you are stuck for advice and God will help you to work things out together with them. So many times you will forget this counsel and wish you asked earlier. Before you despair and get depressed about your situation, give that pastor or Godly friend a ring and ask for help. You have many people around you that love you and want to help you out.

Try not to feel guilty for too long for what you have said and done wrong. Know that God is a forgiving God and that He wants you to get out of bed, say sorry and have another go.

Please listen to this advice and learn these lessons. They will help you to have more joy and peace in your life and help to prevent some of the pain you inevitably have to go through.

From,

Your 57-year-old self

(I met my husband when I was 16. I left school at 15 and was working full time when I met him.)

CHAPTER SIXTEEN

Thine Own Self

'To thine own self be true,' said Polonius from William Shakespeare's play 'Hamlet'.

It seems like a worthy tattoo, a quote to pursue in our life, but honestly it is not great advice from a character who was very immature.

I do believe each and every one of us has a true self that we are designed to both find and create, but the pursuit of narcissism in a society obsessed with selfies is bleak.

I think a greater quote to embrace and make our mantra is this one...

"I am fearfully and wonderfully made; Wonderful are your works; my soul knows it very well."

Psalm 139:14

It connects our true essence, our personality, our uniqueness to a Creator who designed us with intention. There is an essence within every single person that is unique. It is a piece of your soul that no-one knows but God, a creation with likeness to God, but brilliance in our very own uniqueness.

We can be true to the uniqueness of our original design, but also acknowledge it in a way that grounds us in the bigger picture of a plan designed by a creative God. A humble place. An anchor that holds us secure when the storms of life plague. Knowing who we are and what unique signature we were designed to bring to the earth.

One of the greatest pursuits we can commit to in our single season is the discovery of finding truly who we are. Spending hours alone, moments in deep conversation, opportunities of reflection finding out what makes us unique.

The best marriage partners are those who are completely true to themselves. The worst partners are those who carry insecurity, baggage and controlling ways to keep the relationship safe enough to stop their true selves from being discovered.

Who are you?

Are you okay when things are a little unclear?

Do you try to control relationships, friendships, work colleagues, so that you feel safe?

One of the greatest discoveries in my summer of love was the realisation that I often controlled people and situations to make myself feel secure.

I would be the one in charge. I would be the one making the plans and breaking them. As I became more okay with my vulnerabilities and began to trust more people, I started to learn so many things about myself.

Parts of me that I had no idea existed. It is every one of these discoveries that has helped me be a better wife.

Facing my single self and acknowledging who I really was and the areas of my life that I really wanted to change.

This would be the greatest gift anyone could give their future spouse.

Truly knowing who we are and what we have been designed to do.

"In fact a mature person doesn't fall in love, he rises in love. The word fall is not right. Only immature people fall; they stumble and fall down in love, somehow they were managing and standing. They cannot manage and they cannot stand – they find a woman and they are gone, they find a man and they are gone. They were always ready to fall on the ground and to creep. They don't have that integrity to stand alone.

A mature person has the integrity to be alone. And when a mature person gives love, he gives without any strings attached to it: he simply gives. And when a mature person gives love, he feels grateful that you have accepted his love, not vice versa. He does not expect you to be thankful for it – no, not at all, he does not even need your thanks. He thanks you for accepting his love.

And when two mature persons are in love, one of the greatest paradoxes of life happens, one of the most beautiful phenomena: they are together and yet tremendously alone, they are together so much so that they are almost one. But their oneness does not destroy their individuality; in fact, it enhances it: they become more individual. Two mature persons in love help each other to become more free. There is no politics involved, no diplomacy, no effort to dominate. How can you dominate the person you love? Just think over it.

Domination is a sort of hatred, anger, enmity. How can you think of dominating a person you love? You would love to see the person totally free, independent; you will give him more individuality. That's why I call it the greatest paradox: they are together so much so that they are almost one, but still in that oneness they are individuals. Their individualities are not effaced; they have become more enhanced. The other has enriched them as far as their freedom is concerned.

Immature people falling in love destroy each other's freedom, create a bondage, make a prison. Mature persons in love help each other to be free; they help each other to destroy all sorts of bondages. And when love flows with freedom there is beauty. When love flows with dependence there is ugliness."

Osho

14. GO TO THE MOVIES BY YOURSELF.

For most of you, I bet this is not a big deal, but for me I hated going to the movies alone. There was something about sitting in a big old cinema, feeling lonely surrounded by other couples, and groups of friends and family chatting that made me feel even more alone.

The summer when I faced this fear and I just swum in the river upstream, against the tide of people and popcorn, I felt like I had overcome the world.

Going to the movies by yourself might not be a biggie, but what is?

Buying a house by yourself?

Shifting out from your family's home?

Travelling to Europe?

What is the sacred cow, that you will not sacrifice until you are tied?

Maybe it is time to do that very thing you fear. There are many things we can do without needing someone by our side.

Be brave, dear friend.

Dear single self,

Remember how you remind EVERYONE that EVERYTHING happens for a reason! Even when it makes no sense at the time. I know it is hard sometimes and that some days happen without a thought to your 'relationship status', whereas on other days it seems as though it's flashing on your head like a neon light in Vegas for all the world to see.

You know when you're at a family function or gathering meeting new people, you awkwardly find yourself in that room FULL of loved up couples, and newlyweds seem to be multiplying by the minute and you are thinking to yourself, 'why did I come again?' because the first question everyone seems to be asking is, 'are you married? Where is your husband? Oh you're so pretty – why are you single?'

These times WILL come and they are the hardest part of being single, especially as you approach and reach the big 3-0, it's like wedding central. BUT don't get caught up in all the hype. PLEASE remember that God has a divine plan for your life that's perfect for you, no-one else but you.

God showed you that he has a purpose for you and projects he put on your heart and soul by no mistake that he needs you to accomplish first. Before you meet that significant other, KEEP MEDITATING on that promise girl!

You have been in BAD (VERY BAD), destructive, dishonest, unreliable, controlling relationships in the past and now is your time to be a witness to the beauty that can be had in a right relationship, a destined encounter. It will be fruitful, trustworthy, reliable, honest, caring, considerate and EXCEED your expectations in ways you cant even imagine; now THAT is worth waiting for!!! PLEASE DON'T SETTLE FOR ANYTHING LESS THAN THIS.

Never Give Up!! I know you're a hopeless romantic and believe in fairy tales coming true, so be hopeful now! I really feel God is building you up for something great. Keep taking positive steps of faith into living your purpose. Because you don't want to meet someone who doesn't fit into this anyway, right?

For now take advantage of the moments when you can just go for a coffee and relax, eat cereal for dinner, go for a massage, read a book. Plan something without taking anyone else's schedule or opinion into account – do this now. Most importantly, chase your dreams. DO NOT focus on and see marriage as the only purpose to aspire to just because you are a woman! Because you don't have to compromise just yet, enjoy this season. Remember everything in life is for a season; you reached 30 and you thought how fast time actually does go, so embrace it, take the good days with the bad knowing you're living in your moment now. All past moments have gone and who knows what tomorrow may bring.

Don't stop creating, dreaming, hoping and imagining big things because they WILL come. You know this deep down, don't despise the small humble beginnings. Everything starts small and has the potential to grow into something amazing if inspired, encouraged and nurtured in the right way. His timing is perfect – be patient!

The one that God has placed will see YOU, the real you, behind your shyness, nerves, deep thinking, flaws and all. I know it can be incredibly hard and lonely BUT use this time to nurture and grow, honour yourself for being you! Sometimes you may compare yourself to others and wonder why it is not happening to you.

What am I doing wrong?

Is there something wrong with me?

NO NO NO STOP!!!

You are strong and God is with you.

You are not alone, God is with you always. The challenges you face doing this season alone are for a destined purpose and God will restore all you have lost and hardships you endured.

HE will bless you above and beyond. I KNOW THIS!!! If you just trust in him and his plans.

Love from,

The future you who is living the promises.

CHAPTER SEVENTEEN

Babies

When I was five years old, my Mum now tells me I was very dramatic. I would cry on cue, waiting for all the attention, a brilliant actress in the making. We shifted from the city to a little seaside town, during my first term of grade one, primary school.

Every morning I would wake up crying and telling my Mum I didn't want to go to school as I felt sick. She would tell me that I was just acting and send me off to my new school.

One morning she said to me angrily, "Amanda, I will take you to the doctors, just to prove that you are not sick." So off we went, to the doctors, with my doll in tow, dressed in my school uniform, so that Mum could drop me off to school afterwards.

Within a few minutes of speaking to the doctor, my Mum's face went grey, as he told her I needed to go straight to the hospital. He was sure I was very sick. Quickly I was rushed in an ambulance, to Fremantle hospital and then on to the Princess Margaret Hospital for Children.

I had a severe case of appendicitis and my appendix had already burst. It was a really serious condition which, had it not been found within a few hours, my very life was would have been at risk.

The most serious part about this situation was that gangrene had set in and the infection had spread to my ovaries and fallopian tubes.

There I was dressed that morning ready for my school day, then on the operating theatre having three organs removed and in hospital for weeks.

In the midst of this operation I heard doctors, nurses and medical staff talk about my condition. I struggled to understand what they were saying but essentially I had one ovary and one fallopian tube removed, as well as my appendix. The question was whether my other ovary and tube had been affected and this would not be known until it was time for me to start my family.

Fast forward years later, turning twenty-five, turning twenty-nine, turning thirty-two, my heart would sink every birthday wondering whether I would ever be able to have my own family.

You see women are born with all the eggs they need in their lives to have a family. We don't grow or produce eggs, we are born with them. So being one ovary down, meant my egg count was halved already. Then each year we get older, the eggs diminish and every year over the age of thirty, the chances of falling pregnant diminishes. Year after year.

I got married at 35, unsure that I would fall pregnant. I got married to a man who was willing to walk the course of this journey with me. Six months before we got married, I went to my local doctor and said I was getting married in the next six months and wanted to go on the pill.

That doctor's appointment was the most demeaning and terrible appointment of my life. I sat with a woman I had gone to many times before and she just looked at me and said, "You are over 35, Amanda. You should not go on the pill, you should be trying to get pregnant straight away. The likelihood is very slim anyway."

I remember walking out of the surgery with tears streaming down my face, knowing I had to talk to my fiancé about this again, thinking he is not going to marry someone who can't have children.

I rang him straight away and he said this: "We will go to another doctor, we will go on the pill and give ourselves a year of being married and if God wants us to have a baby, he will do it despite the pill." A man of courage, a man of faith.

True to his word, six weeks into being married, six weeks of being together as husband and wife, whilst on the contraceptive pill, one unsuspecting Monday morning, my brand new husband was under the kitchen sink, fixing a leak in our new house, and I walked from the bathroom carrying a pregnancy test, with a positive reading on it.

We both looked at each other completely shocked. Despite the pill, which is 99% effective as a contraceptive, despite the fact that I was turning 36 that year, despite the fact that I had only one ovary and fallopian tube, I was indeed pregnant.

A little miracle to celebrate our newly formed family. A huge change for us to come to terms with in the first year of our marriage. The most amazing endeavour of our whole life.

That February, I gave birth to my son Maximus, and two years later, gave birth to a little girl we named Liberty.

My story is unique to our circumstances, but I never gave up believing that God is indeed faithful to the promises that he gives us and the desires of our hearts.

Many years I waited, afraid and concerned that I would never become a mother and here I type today with a little girl sleeping beside me and a toddler asleep in the next room. Life unfolded quickly before me after years and years of waiting.

15. START A JOURNAL FOR YOUR FUTURE HUSBAND?

One of the greatest ways that I processed the despair of my waiting was continually finding ways to keep my heart hopeful.

It sounds a little random, but during the times I felt most despondent, the days that I thought I would never get married, the days I thought I would never have children or a family, I wrote.

I wrote in a book.

Some journal pages have been since ripped out, because honestly no-one needed to read them, but most of them I found myself writing to my future husband and reminding myself of all the things I believed that one day would come true.

On our wedding day, I woke up to a tree. A beautiful sterling silver tree, covered in little cards and notes from my husband to me on our wedding day. Precious little encouragements to remind me how much he adored me and I gave him a leather parcel containing a gathering of letters and journal entries, musings on days when I believed he was far from reality, prayers about him wherever he was, moments waiting to meet him and continue on our lives together.

Some people might think this is a little desperate and I'm sure some of you are thinking, "what if I never get married?"

I believe that if it is a desire of your heart, I believe if it is a dream, I believe if it is a deep longing, that it will indeed be fulfilled.

I will believe that for you, even on the days that you cannot believe it for yourself.

I believe that God delights in giving us the desires of our hearts.

Writing and speaking out those longings is a great part of building your faith and belief too.

Dear single self,

Your early childhood has been very beautiful. One of safety, love, animals, adventure and make believe.

It was only in your later teenage years that that stability and life as you knew it was rocked violently by politics, war, fear, divorce and confusion. This created an instability and struggle which you had never experienced before as it rudely broke into your idyllic, happy world. It catapulted you into a desire to run, to create for yourself a different life, a life of adventure and of forgetting. You vowed to yourself that you would never allow another person to feel the pain that you felt.

Marriage and motherhood had never been your goals or your plans for the future. You'd always been content to play with animals and to help people. You cared deeply about people in pain. You wanted always to fix broken hearts, give hope and make them happy again. Your favourite stories have always had that common theme.

Arriving in England aged 20 in your quest for adventure was exciting and liberating but there was little wisdom. You lived plastically for the moment with little regard for your future self. It was during this time that you met your future husband. Were you secure? No. Did you know who you really were? No. Could you have in all reality sat down and written your future self a letter at that point? I don't think you could've. I don't think you had the wisdom. I don't think you knew what you wanted.

Today, as a mature woman in God, I could look back and think of what I would have liked to say at that point. But I didn't say it then.

So what would I say?

You have been born into a beautiful family. You are deeply loved. Your mother and father wanted you desperately and awaited your birth with great expectation. Between the birth of your brother and your own birth, your mother experienced ten miscarriages. You were waited for for a very long time. There was much rejoicing when you were born. You were played with, celebrated, believed in, kissed, hugged and enjoyed. You had a wonderful foundation on which to build. Never forget that.

Honour your parents. Celebrate them. Write them a letter and tell them how much you appreciate all they did for you, all they sacrificed for you. How you treat relationships past will translate into relationships future.

Life will not always be easy. Life will not always hand you things on a plate. You will sometimes have to face tragedies and make difficult choices which may cause you pain. Never forget your beginnings. Never forget you are loved and believed in despite harsh seasons which try to force you to shrink.

A time will come when the One who created you will call your name. Respond. Allow Him to do in you all that He wills. He will lift up that bowed head, kiss away your tears and give you a hope for a future you never imagined. He will teach you how to love. Don't allow this moment to pass you by. It is the most important moment of your future. Wait expectantly for it. Your future is dependant on that moment.

Rise up and live an overcoming life. Rise to every occasion, smile at the future, live courageously despite that medical report, that overwhelming pain, that thing that tries to destroy you. There is One who watches you, who gives you hope when there is no hope, who whispers to you when you can't hear for the noise. Believe that whisper and follow that voice.

Love others extravagantly and live generously. Nothing will give you more joy. Celebrate people and never compare yourself with others. In the giving away you will receive so much more. Take special care that you never let what you get out of the giving be the reason for your generosity, love or extravagance. Be surprised by anything that comes back. It will always take your breath away.

Develop your character. Live a life which speaks to those around you. Live a life others want to follow. A life that is healing to those around you. A life that brings peace. Enjoy your life. Don't let moments pass you by. Notice the twinkle in that eye, the desperation in that voice, the heart longing to know more. Don't be so caught up in your own life and agenda that you miss the moment. Life is full of them. Take the time to become all that God has for you. He knows you best. Live in His grip of grace. His grace drenched love. It is then that you will become that loving wife, that irresistible Mum, that loyal friend, that courageous overcomer.

Your past matters, your present matters, your future matters. Take the happy parts of your past to build on the present to take into the future. Forgive what caused you pain. Forgive yourself.

Live a life without regrets. Life is too short to do otherwise. Drink tea in the garden, admire creation, appreciate beauty. Celebrate and spend lots of time with those you love.

Your future is a blank canvas. Paint something inspiring and beautiful. The world and your future self is waiting.

Forever Loved,

Me (Married at 23. Now 58.)

CHAPTER EIGHTEEN

Broken Crayons

The year I turned twenty-one was the worst year of my life. Studying Music Theatre at the Western Australian Academy of Performing Arts (WAAPA); I also owned a business teaching dancing, theatre and singing. I was living the life of my childhood dreams.

Two thousand people applied for that University course while I was accepted with a small group of less than twenty people. My business was thriving, I couldn't keep up with the students and the opportunities. I was offered a role in a professional musical playing at His Majesty's Theatre in Perth.

Everyone watching on would have thought I was blissfully loving life.

I was a great actor however.

There were moments of beauty, creativity and outrageous expression, but internally I was completely overwhelmed by the difficulty of my circumstances that year.

All I wanted was to be loved.

All I wanted was for a knight in shining armour to come and whisk me away.

All I wanted was not the life I was living.

It honestly made no sense, I had achieved everything my teenage heart had dreamed and longed for but I was broken.

In that ensuing year, my parents divorced after 21 years of marriage, also one of my closest friends committed suicide and my Nanna, the matriarch of our family, suddenly died of pneumonia.

Personally, that season of my life was the most devastating year, but it was also the most defining. I felt like I was drowning even though there was no water.

I just wanted to take a breath, I just wanted someone to rescue me, I was desperate.

You know what though – despite the devastation I carried on creating, writing and expressing my innovation and creativity.

I found ways to express my heartache and to gradually redefine what I thought was important.

I found over that season of grief, sadness and desperation broken crayons still colour.

As a young girl I remember lining up all my crayons ready to express myself and draw my little masterpiece. If one of the crayons was broken, I felt unable to finish my art work and was often very disappointed.

As an adult I have discovered that broken crayons still colour.

No matter the seasons of brokenness, we still have something to contribute and a hope for the future to hold onto.

It was just before Christmas after the craziest eighteen months of my young life that I realised something needed to drastically change so that I could pursue those things that were for me in a new season.

Something had to change.

After finishing university, I gave up my business and wrote a letter of resignation to my employers. I signed up for Bible College starting the next term and I packed up my car and shifted to the city.

A new season unfolded quite radically for me that summer. I made decisions to start again, even though my life looked like I had had everything completely under control.

This little broken crayon began her life again.

It was one of the best decisions I have ever made in my life, but one of the most humbling decisions to start again.

New friends, New house, New course, New.

I began again. Even though I had studied two degrees at university and I had run a successful business, I radically surrendered my life to find another.

And that I did.

How about you?

Do you feel like a broken crayon?

Keep colouring my friend, a new blank page maybe awaiting your new season.

"Continue to share your heart with people even if it has been broken."

Amy Poehler

16. BUY A PACKET OF CRAYONS AND COLOUR IN

I have found that some of the most lucid moments in my life are those when I am doing something from my childhood.

Colouring in, fishing on the beach, building a cubby, playing with play dough, sitting in the sand at the beach and building sand castles.

There is something so grounding when we remind ourselves of the simplicity of childhood emotions. When we are excited in summer to taste that first lick of a ice-cream, the first breath taken as we swing on a playground, moments of exhilaration when we jump puddles.

Today I am encouraging you to do something you haven't done in a long time and see what thoughts arise.

Maybe you just need to break a crayon and colour in anyway.

Dear single self,

21 and married... 32 and divorced ...

Take a deep breath; this is not what I planned by any means.

Being single again brings so much perspective and clarity; it's almost like getting a second chance. Looking back I can see how the choices I made were not always in my best interest. You know, things like trying to find my validation and worth in the arms of a man. (This can only be found in the realisation that I am a daughter of the King!)

Or expecting a man to be the one to fix the broken pieces of my heart. (This is the reason Jesus went to the Cross!). Maybe it was the way I took myself into relationships being only half of who I was meant to be. (The wonder of the Cross is that I'm healed and made whole!)

Perhaps it was the destructive self-loathing that unintentionally pushed love away for fear of being hurt. (If Jesus died for me, doesn't that show that I am indeed loveable and should therefore love or at least like myself!)

Divorce hurts (understatement!).

The weight of it is suffocating.

The shame of it is crippling.

And in the early days it felt like a death.

Before I was married, and even just after my divorce, I thought that being single meant I wasn't good enough. But now I see how being single has given me a greater sense of freedom and self-discovery. It's allowed me a chance to grow and draw nearer to God.

The greatest legacy of love from my marriage is continued through the hearts of two most precious blessings that call me Mum. They challenge me to face the future with hope and remind me that my story is not over, the journey is calling and as I venture forward I am cheering you on my dear Single Self.

But this is what I know now. This is what I hope saves you from the brokenness and heartache I've felt. I am a daughter of the King, I am royalty, and that is where my validation and worth is found.

There is One Man who can fix all the broken pieces of my heart, His name is Jesus, and what He did for me in the name of love brings healing and wholeness like nothing else. And if this Man,

Jesus, loves me so much that He would show it by dying upon a Cross, then how can I not see that I am indeed loveable, how can I not at least begin to try to love myself.

The weight of divorce is indeed suffocating. It's dark and scary, it brings loneliness and longing, the shame feels crippling, but from experience I've seen that from the ashes, He brings forth great beauty. My marriage didn't last, but there is beauty in those two most precious hearts who call me Mum.

I trust in His mercies being new every morning and I face my future with hope and joy ... My story has not finished, the journey continues. You need to find your true worth and value in the One who created you. Looking for a man to validate you and fill the void inside is not the answer. It's a lovely sentiment to think that meeting a guy and falling in love will fix everything. I remember the days when I saw roses and rainbows and love hearts – oh my!

You've been approaching love all wrong. The love He has for you cannot compare to any other love this world can offer. Yes, earthly love is grand; it sends you spinning out of control. When you allow His great love to fill you, the overflow will teach you how to truly love another.

If you won't love yourself for who God created you to be, then trust me when I tell you, this destructive self-loathing will inhibit the way a man can love you. Unintentionally you will push him away toward other things, and the agony will wound you ... love yourself, so he can love you.

Allow God to heal your wounds and don't depend on a man to do it.

You will feel deep sorrow.

You will lament and cry out.

Your marriage will breakdown.

You will feel the weight of divorce.

And for a time, you will withdraw and feel completely lost.

The shame is not worth holding.

You are loved,

Me

CHAPTER NINETEEN

A Kind Human

How is your 'perfect guy' list going?

In my late teens I dated a drummer, a surfer and then a designer and, as a single young adult, I dreamed about dating a business man, an innovator, a preacher, a coffee drinker or a writer.

I think I even thought my husband would be a crazy mix of all of these.

One thing I knew deep in my heart though was that he would wear glasses. It's so funny, if a guy wearing glasses even spoke to me for just a minute, my heart slightly melted.

Year after year, I searched for my cafe loving hipster with deep dark framed eyes and I came up very short.

The list that I had floating around my head was becoming like a chain around my neck getting heavier and heavier.

New Year's Eve after New Year's Eve, I stood staring out at the fireworks, watching lovers kiss in the new season, feeling so very sad. Where was this elusive man of my dreams? The little list of attributes I longed for grew and grew.

After years of desperation, and silently appraising the guys that I met, I gave up. I was sick of hoping they may even tick off one or two of the attributes that made up my perfect match.

That elusive list of characteristics that I desired in a partner for life became a heavy cross to carry. I realised one day that I was looking for just one thing.

I wanted to find a kind human.

I wanted to spend the rest of my life with a guy that was kind.

Often we are distracted by the appeal of nice clothing, fancy jobs, impressive titles, with a car to match. As women, we are appalled when men are superficial in their pursuit of beauty, but we are often silent in our judgement of men.

Lately I have been listening a lot to a song by Ed Sheeran, 'Thinking Out Loud'. The lyrics start like this...

"When your legs don't work like they used to before

And I can't sweep you off of your feet

Will your mouth still remember the taste of my love?

Will your eyes still smile from your cheeks?

And, darling, I will be loving you 'til we're 70

And, baby, my heart could still fall as hard at 23

And I'm thinking 'bout how people fall in love in mysterious ways

Maybe just the touch of a hand

Well, me, I fall in love with you every single day

And I just wanna tell you I am"

I am obsessed with the lyrics of this song, because the only thing that matters when we are seventy are the moments of kindness that we have extended to each other during our seasons of challenge.

When our legs don't work anymore, and we can't sweep each other off our feet, what matters is kindness and the memories we have created together.

One of the strongest attributes of the man I married is his kindness. In the days when I am sleep deprived from the intense struggle of a newborn, or those moments when I am desperately deep in thought as I process the depths and heights of life, he is kind.

He is so patient and loving. He cares more about me than anyone else in the world and this indeed matters.

If you have a list that is nearly impossible for anyone to meet, may I offer a suggestion?

What about just looking for someone who is kind?

What about allowing the awkward, socially inept guy to have a chance?

You never know, he may be your perfect match.

Never in my wildest dreams did I think I would marry a body builder; a guy ten years younger than me was never on my dating desirable list but guess what? The day I met him he was wearing glasses (now that is a brilliant story!) and his mum is an optometrist. Hilarious.

He is the kindest human I know and as a father, a husband and a best friend that is indeed a trait worth pursuing.

17. BURN THE LIST

What are the traits or characteristics you have looked for in a partner?

I think there was a teaching that went around a few years ago that told us to write a list and pray, hope, beg that person into being. I have realised in my own experience that this is really unhelpful.

I am challenging you to burn the list.

Not literally (although maybe you have it written down somewhere), but find a way to explore the possibility of a person being perfect for you who may never tick all the bullet points on your list.

Then write one word.

Just one word that is not negotiable.

Mine was kind.

What is yours?

Dear single self,

I was married at 19 and I am now 36.

You may not know this now but there is so much you can do, so many skills to learn, so many friends to make and cherish, a world to explore! It's so easy to think we need a man to lean on, that we are not complete until we find 'the one' but in reality we have to be whole within ourselves to be able to give of ourselves wholeheartedly!

Be confident in yourself and find your own way. Having been married for almost 17 years now, I realise I had to do a lot of my growing up as a married woman. That hasn't always been easy. I have had to learn to be more independent because in many ways I'd never had to be completely. I drove the car my husband had bought, I lived in the house my husband owned, I let him manage the finances and relied on him to be the strong one. Sure I went to university and built a career. I found my way, but I had to learn responsibility the hard way sometimes.

Cherish those who love you, cherish your beautiful friendships. It was easy at 19 to think that I'd found the love of my life and I didn't need anybody else. Many of my friends must have felt like they'd been dissed. Good friends can be good friends for life, no matter what changes. They will add value to you, your future husband and your marriage. We were not made to run the course without friends. They are so important.

Looking back, I have no regrets.

Life is what you make it.

Whatever circumstance you find yourself in, embrace it, work it, grow from it.

We only have one life to live!

Love Me.

CHAPTER TWENTY

Lonely

Some of the loneliest people I know are those who are constantly surrounded by people. The very definition of the word makes us believe that, to be lonely, we must spend a lot of time alone; however, in my experience, this is untrue.

Loneliness is a disease that eats away at our hearts in our over connected, over saturated society.

One of my friends recently wrote on Facebook this status update; "I have at last got to 1,000 friends here on Facebook, but I would be lucky if I actually see three of them regularly." His honesty and vulnerability stopped my scrolling hand. I read between the lines of his declaration and he was saying, "I am lonely. I have many people who call me acquaintance but hardly any who call me friend."

How about you? If you were honest, is this how you feel about your place in our online world?

It is bizarre, we are sharing more of our intimate moments with more people than ever before, people voyeuristically watch our big moments unfold in real time, but we are often overwhelmed with loneliness. I remember lying in bed late at night desperately feeling completely misunderstood and alone.

I remember moments of being surround by hundreds of people at events when I was working and unsure if anyone actually noticed or cared about me.

Loneliness is not about how many people are around you or how many people you interact with. Often single people believe that 'If only I just could get married, then I wouldn't be lonely anymore.' I have found in my life however, some of the loneliest people can be those who are married. This is because loneliness is not an external physical condition of how many people we surround ourselves with; it is an internal expression of how you feel inside.

Finding ways to express these feelings of aloneness is a really important step towards feeling connected. Unless we are truly honest about how we feel and find someone or something to help us process these emotions, we will never find a place of acceptance, even if we are surrounded by people who love us.

Does loneliness overwhelm you? Then take time to find a way to reach out and ask someone to help you process these very valid feelings.

"Here's to the people who try their hardest to be good enough for everyone; who spend hours reading random quotes to find the right one; who listen to the same song dozens of times because the lyrics mean a lot; who deserve so much more than they get and are willing to fight for it and those who wished upon a star, wasted on someone that will never care; and to the beautiful people that feel lonely in their heart."

Brigitte Nicole

18. WRITE A LIST OF WHAT MAKES YOU FEEL MOST CONNECTED.

What truly makes you feel the happiest?

When you are in a big group of people laughing?

When you are having coffee with one great friend who you feel deeply connected with?

When you are helping or serving others?

Shopping?

Drawing?

Write a list of the things that truly fuel you and make you come alive relationally.

Now on the same piece of paper, write a list of the things that make you feel the most alone… a list of things that really drain you.

Your challenge is to do something from the list that makes you feel most connected this week.

Little changes that will make a big difference.

Dear single self,

Oh my, does God have an incredible plan for you!

I know you're wondering if God has forgotten you ... never been kissed, never had a boyfriend ... and you're asking yourself, 'What's wrong with me?' Such confusion and disappointment, heartache and tears.

Let me tell you that through these single years you are going to connect deeply with your family and meet kind natured and loyal friends. These relationships are going to keep you centred on God and open your eyes to the beautiful world around you.

Most importantly, though, you are going to get to know your Creator. The One who loves you unconditionally and, best of all, He's the author of your life. You'll look back and see that God's timing is and was perfect.

Fall in love with the One who first loved you. Talk to Him openly and honestly. Share your dreams with Him. He loves spending time with you.

Don't waste your days. Seize every opportunity.

Figure out what you've been created for and spend time with family and friends. Intentional time.

Cherish the stories and the moments.

Then, because you invested in relationships and prioritised Him, your heart will be ready to meet the most caring, selfless, Jesus loving man. A man that pursues you and tells you that he loves you and that he thinks you're beautiful ... every day! A man that honours you, your family and friends. A man that is courageous and thoughtful and a friend always. A man that loves his Creator. A man that you fall more deeply in love with each day.

These relationships will be celebrated on your wedding day. Your best friends and family will laugh, cry, worship God, and dance the night away with you. You wouldn't change the events that lead you to this day for the world. You will be incredibly grateful that you kept yourself pure and waited, even when you didn't understand why? Guard your heart and treat yourself and others with respect.

Don't be anxious about anything. Put aside your people pleasing ways. Let go of your unrealistic expectations and embrace the plan God has for you.

Your life will be full of blessings. Your family will remain beside you, your friends will be loyal. You will cherish your husband. He will be your best friend and you will have incredible adventures together. Most of all you will cherish your Creator who knows you intimately.

Love me

(I was married at 24 and am now 26. I was very single until the age of 21. My husband is the first and only man that has ever kissed me and my one and only boyfriend and husband.)

"Too many girls rush into relationships because of the fear of being single, then start making compromises, and losing their identity. Don't do that."

Katy Perry

CHAPTER TWENTY ONE

Adventure

One of the greatest moments in my Summer of Love was the time that I flew into Bangkok by myself at 2 o'clock in the morning.

I felt overwhelmingly scared but truly alive. I had never been to Thailand before, but I knew a huge part in discovering who I was and falling in love with my own uniqueness was putting myself in situations I had never been in before. I had always been a bit of a control freak and trust was a big issue back then.

I was a workaholic, obsessed with what people thought about me. I was creative, volatile, and my love of people was deeply heartfelt.

I needed a break to discover myself, I needed to recover some of what I had lost during the pursuit of keeping others happy. I needed an adventure of epic proportions, so that is what I did.

I packed up a little bag, booked my ticket to Thailand, Dubai, Lebanon and off I flew.

I was terrified.

I was more engaged in life than I had ever been.

I was on the edge of my dirty aeroplane seat.

As I walked out of customs, preparing myself to go to my first guest house, I took a deep breath of the thick air and just jumped in a taxi.

True adventure awakens the gift of being present. I had realised that I was living in the future and waiting for a husband in order to do the things I dreamed of. I wanted to travel the world, but I wanted to wait to do it with my husband.

The crazy thing is, now that I am married with two children, flying off to foreign lands and putting myself in precarious situations is the furthest thing from my mind.

One day again I will pull on my crazy backpacking travel boots, but for now home is where my heart is and if I hadn't embraced the moment and travelled back then, I know I would find myself in a place of regret today.

What adventure plagues your dreams?

What crazy places, far off universes do you think about discovering?

Do it.

Plan that adventure, book that ticket, become an interesting person, with crazy and outrageous risk taking stories. Live the life you dream of living today.

Live without regrets.

The stories I have to tell from the year of travel that followed are outrageous. Stories of being stopped by the military in Lebanon who did not want to let me get through to a village, stories of being pulled over in America for driving on the wrong side of the road. Stories of being kicked off a plane on a tarmac in London bound for Paris, to being caught in a fire in a slum in the middle of Bangkok.

Adventure is awaiting discovery, you just need to be brave enough to embrace it.

What adventure is awaiting you?

Pursue it.

"Let us step into the night and pursue that flighty temptress, adventure."

J.K. Rowling

19. BOOK A HOLIDAY.

When was the last time you took a decent holiday? Do you have a big pile of leave sitting in your HR office? Do you holiday often but always at the same place, with the same people?

My challenge is for you to plan a holiday to a far off destination or, if you travel often and widely, to plan a stay-cation in your own city.

Read travel blogs, look at hotel reviews, find tours to go on, look into the history of the nations.

Get interested in something that is outside your everyday.

Recently we had a stay-cation in our own city and it was amazing. It is all about planning to do something that you don't normally do and get yourself out of your comfort zone.

Plan an adventure. If you feel lonely and travelling by yourself is too much, book a cruise or a tour, so you can meet new people.

You know you want to.

Write to me and let me know where you are going, I am sure I will be a little jealous.

Dear single self,

I am now 49 years old. I married at 20 and found myself single again at 28. I now have two experiences of singleness, and two very different experiences they are.

I guess it would be wisest to first address my younger single self. What can I say to you? How can I encourage you? How can I explain what I've gleaned over the years to guide you through your singleness?

Firstly, I want to encourage you to just enjoy being young. Get out with your friends, experience life. Follow your dreams and stop worrying what people will think of you. Don't rush your life, don't be in a hurry to grow up. Don't try to fill the voids in your life through whatever alternatives are placed in front of you. God is the only one who can fill that void. I know you're scared but if you give God a chance some time, you will learn not to be so afraid and, even when you are, God will be there with you.

Getting married is something special. It is the union of two people who truly love one another and want to grow together forever. Marriage isn't an escape from a life that you find you don't fit into. Spend time with people, both male and female; about relationships, invest in relationships. Risk being vulnerable and transparent. Not everyone is out to hurt you.

Please learn who you are, what you love and desire and what makes you happy. Stop trying to please everyone around you and be a little selfish sometimes. Take your feelings into account and push for what you want occasionally.

Life is meant to be lived – not regretted.

And then to my older single self. Don't see yourself as a failure. You have grown since you married and gave birth to your beautiful sons. Don't view yourself so harshly. Don't act like your life is over. Enjoy those children God has given you to raise. Invest in them. Teach them. Show them how to be resilient, to rise above the circumstances that life dishes out.

Stop assuming you know what others are thinking about you. Give people a chance. Don't hang onto the hurt of one person and blame everyone. Don't let that one person stop you from having a fulfilling single life.

You are valuable whether you are in a relationship or not. You have so much to offer people but they will never know until you let go of your pain so you can trust them. Take chances. Accept that pain and hurt occur but know that if you can just change your perspective, you will see that there are some genuine people out there who want to get to know you.

Let down you walls, unwrap your heart, open your eyes, get out of the house, pray and trust that the God who created you is with you and loves you.

Stop expecting others to make a life for you. Get off the couch, get out of the house and take some risks.

Learn to love yourself so that others can love you too.

Love

Me

CHAPTER TWENTY TWO

Love

In my journey over that summer of self discovery, I believe I learnt one the greatest lessons of my whole life – how to love.

There have been many books about love, there have been many movies about love, but I have realised that it is difficult to love another, when we do not know how to love ourselves.

Finding ways to learn how to process my emotions and be content with who I was took me on a journey of discovery that summer that no-one could have ever predicted.

I read a quote recently that said this;

> *"Most of my life has been spent trying to shrink myself. Trying to become smaller. Quieter. Less sensitive. Less opinionated. Less needy. Less me. Because I didn't want to be a burden. I didn't want to be too much or push people away. I wanted people to like me. I wanted to be cared for and valued. I wanted to be wanted. So for years, I sacrificed myself for the sake of making other people happy. And for years, I suffered. But I'm tired of suffering, and I'm done shrinking. It's not my job to change who I am in order to become someone else's idea of a worthwhile human being. I am worthwhile. Not because other people think I am, but because I exist, and therefore I matter. My thoughts matter. My feelings matter. My voice matters. And with or without anyone's permission or approval, I will continue to be who I am and speak my truth. Even if it makes people angry. Even if*

it makes them uncomfortable. Even if they choose to leave. I refuse to shrink. I choose to take up space. I choose to honour my feelings. I choose to give myself permission to get my needs met. I choose to make self-care a priority. I choose me."

Daniell Koepke

Self care is an unusual combination of words. We often are so worried about everyone else, that looking after ourselves becomes low on the priority lists.

Self care is not selfishness. I am not suggesting that you become narcissistic and unable to help or care about anyone but yourself. I am suggesting that you take time to fill your love tank up with things that matter to you alone.

Do you love to walk the ocean, but don't because it seems overly romantic?

Do it. Book a date with yourself.

Do you love to have a bath, with candles, music and a glass of wine?

Make it happen.

Do you love to travel, does it make you feel alive?

Book that ticket, even alone.

Do you want to buy a house and make it the most beautiful home?

Make plans, make a budget, get going.

Stop waiting for someone else to love. Begin to love yourself through self care. Find ways to honour your feelings, being mindful of that which makes you thrive and do it.

Love yourself as much as you seek love and as much as you love others.

Fill your diary with moments of beauty that deeply impact your soul.

Find a creative gang that you can throw around brilliant ideas with, go to the movies with a young person in your sphere and look at the experience through their eyes.

Live large and love extravagantly.

Love is not the reserve of the candlelit dinner for two. It is an extravagant response to a loving relationship with your Creator, available for everyone.

You are loved and you are worthy of love.

Love large my friend.

Love deep.

Don't be afraid to love you.

The very core of who you are.

" 'i love myself.'
the quietest.
simplest.
mostpowerful.
revolution.
ever."

Nayyirah Waheed

20. CAFE CONVERSATION; SELF CARE.

When I write the words 'self care' what is the image that first comes to you?

A weird ritual from the self help section of the Library?

Something a psychologist says in passing conversation to sound intelligent?

Self care is simply a list of nurturing things that make you feel loved and well. Each and every one of us expresses love in a unique way and receives love in different ways as well.

As a single woman, it is easy to stop caring and loving ourselves because we are so busy trying to escape the feelings that often overwhelm us.

Write a list of things that make you feel loved. Here are some ideas:

Bath

Movies

Dinner with friends

Presents

Time

Jobs ticked off a list

Massage

Deep conversation

Then organise to have a coffee and conversation with a good friend about these things.

Sometimes all it takes is a conversation that matters to open up your heart to the possibility of loving differently and extravagantly.

How can you love yourself more?

"Love yourself. Forgive yourself. Be true to yourself. How you treat yourself sets the standard for how others will treat you."

Steve Maraboli

Dear single self,

I love you.

You will be loved as intensely as you love.

Life can be just as wonderful being single as it is as a couple. You will be married before 30 – 26 in fact, and have your first beautiful baby two days before your 29th birthday. Life is grand.

I wish worry free nights for you; all the hours wasted perusing those who don't have the same beliefs as you are detrimental to your self worth. You are made in the image of God and His love is all you need.

As soon as you let go the obsession with 'needing' to find a husband and embrace what God had planned for you – even if that means living a single life – you will truly be freed. That is when you will meet him.

Love God, yourself, your friends and family. Travel. Laugh. Love without expectation.

Love from a Woman / Wife / Mother / You. (29)

CHAPTER TWENTY THREE

The in-between

Most nights this summer, as I have seen a flash of pink hit the sky, we have run out to our little position on the stairs and watched the sun say goodbye to the day. Lately there have been many bush fires, so the sunsets have been somewhat bittersweet. The bush fire smoke throws a pretty amazing filter over what would already be a beautiful sunset on our Shoalwater Beach.

Every night as the sun slinks behind the sea though, there is this moment of nothing that lasts a good minute before the throw of colour hits the sky canvas. As I wait there for the colour to come, it is so easy to turn and walk away. The one minute seems so much longer than it actually is.

Many people take photos of the sun circle half dipping into the ocean and others of the purple and pink paint thrown across the sky, but no-one really notices the space of the in-between. No-one really notices because they are waiting for the flashes of colour to appear. They have a hope that the aftermath of the sun setting will be as beautiful as the time before. Moments of beauty mixed with moments of waiting.

This week I have had many conversations with people who are tired of the in-between. They so desperately want to move forward into the future and live the life they are dreaming of, but they are stuck in this place of in-between. Waiting for something we desire so deeply is a difficult season in our lives.

A lot of the conversations I have had this week have been with people wanting to get married and they have been waiting for a long time.

The in-between.

How do we carry ourselves during the in-between moments of life?

When we are applying for jobs and they just don't pull of?

When we so desperately want to change our status from single to married?

When we want to start a family and the second little line just doesn't want to appear?

The in-between.

It is a terribly vulnerable place to stand, looking into the distance waiting for the colours of the picture you have of your life. It is easier to believe that it is just not going to happen and to turn and walk away. It is easier to stop hoping than to stay stuck in a place when the deferral constantly makes your heart sick.

In my seasons of waiting, I have had some years when I have done it well and other times I just got sad, angry and completely over it.

The one thing I was determined to do though was to never give up in that in-between place. I never walked away. Even when my hope was at its lowest, I still faced the mountain before me and believed that there was some way through.

Finding friends who would stand and pray with me. Chatting with counsellors and using writing as a therapy to process and let go of the disappointment and anger. Staying in that uncomfortable place of expectation no matter the years I waited. Reaffirming myself with promises and dreams that tarried.

Whether it is a job, a husband, a realisation of a career you've longed for, a change in circumstances, a family. I acknowledge the pain you are feeling in that in-between place. I am asking you to turn and face the horizon though and look for new and beautiful colours to return again.

Have you stopped believing that your dream of better days could come true?

Are you despising every part of that in-between place?

What can you do to dig deep and find the purpose in this place?

"For a long time it had seemed to me that life was about to begin—real life. But there was always some obstacle in the way. Something to be got through first, some unfinished business, time still to be served, a debt to be paid. Then life would begin. At last it dawned on me that these obstacles were my life."

Alfred Souza

21. WHAT HAVE YOU BEEN WAITING FOR?

Is there anything you have been waiting for that you could actually do today?

You know what it is.

The first thing that came to your mind?

How about sitting down and making a plan towards doing it.

Like buying that house.

Parachuting out of that plane.

Going on that holiday.

Find one thing on your bucket list and start to make plans towards doing it this year.

Dear single self,

There is something I want to tell you. I know the loneliness and hopelessness is palpable right now, I remember it vividly, but I want to share something with you. Life can also be amazing if you let it. I got married just after my 36th birthday and I am now 37 turning 38. And you want to know the best thing of all?

I fell in love with and got to marry my best friend.

I know this easy for me to say in hindsight, but can you do something really simple for me? I want you to start caring for yourself. The most crucial piece of advice I ever received was to focus on one thing at a time, de-clutter and simplify my world. Stop stretching and craving and chasing after what is beyond you at this moment. Start to live your life, live it and wholeheartedly enjoy it.

So, go and figure out what it is that makes you happy, forgive yourself for making mistakes, stop being that hermit, go out with friends and be brave. Do things that you are afraid of doing. Guess what? You survive! Become that woman who is deeply content and happy ... with her own company.

Life is not perfectly scripted like the movies. It's messy and forever changing. No-one ever gets it right first time, every time (because that would be really boring!).

One thing I cannot tell you ... The yearning for that baby has not been fulfilled yet. When I thought I would never marry, I mourned over the possibility of never having a child. I don't have the power to predict that for us, all I can say is that I am at peace with what God brings us.

Last of all, but by no means least, when your future husband learns that he is the only man you have ever kissed, that is the most wonderful and freeing sensation. Please don't lessen that honour by thinking it's something to be ashamed of. You made that decision early on and I know sometimes you think it's not worth holding onto ... But believe me it is, and you will NEVER regret it.

Love future me.

CHAPTER TWENTY FOUR

Learning to say No

Over the last twenty-something chapters of this book, I have been trying to get you to say yes. Asking you to mix it up. Saying yes to opportunities, getting yourself in new spaces, new friendships. Stepping into the uncomfortable to open your heart and life up to new possibilities. Sometimes, though, we say no to things when we should say yes, and conversely we say yes to things when we should be saying no.

Confused?

I have found in my life it was often easier to just say yes rather than no to distracting things.

As a mother.

As a friend.

As a lover.

As a mentor.

Lately I have been really aware of how often I used to say yes to something when I knew in my season I should have just said no.

No to long periods of time on social media.

No to worrying about what people think of me.

No to full time work opportunities that take me away from my family.

No to my toddler, even when a melt down is likely to ensue.

Some call it boundaries, some call it protective behaviour, but for me it's actually so I can say yes to the things I know I am meant to be focussing on for the season I am in.

Yes, to exercise.

Yes, to writing.

Yes, to time focused on my family.

Yes, to my friends who engage and want to be part of my life.

Yes.

I cannot say yes to these things, important opportunities, if I don't say no to that which distracts me.

Sometimes we get a little stuck and are unable to see breakthrough in our everyday because we are saying yes to the wrong things. Then sometimes we say no to the right things and the opportunities pass us by.

Are you saying yes to work and no to social opportunities where you can meet new people?

Do you say yes to helping someone and then no to spending time with friends, church, events where you may meet someone new, because you are exhausted?

Do you say yes to the television and no to a date because you just can't be bothered?

What are you saying yes to, that you know in your heart of hearts that you shouldn't?

Maybe it's your season like mine to start saying no a little more, so we can say yes to that which should be our priority.

"Take a shower, wash off the day.
Drink a glass of water.
Make the room dark.
Lie down and close your eyes.
Notice the silence.
Notice your heart.
Still beating.
Still fighting.
You made it, after all.
You made it, another day.
And you can make it one more.
You're doing just fine."

Charlotte Eriksson

22. OBLIGATIONS VERSUS OPPORTUNITY.

We all have obligations, but what if your life is full of so many obligations that you are unable to say yes to new opportunities?

When I say the word obligation, what is the first thing that comes to mind?

Take time to write in your journal about this obligation and why you are finding it draining in this season.

What can you do to say no to some obligations to open up space for more opportunities?

> *"I want to wake up every day and do whatever comes in my mind, and not feel pressure or obligations to do anything else in my life."*
>
> *Michael Jordan*

Dear single self,

You have been beautifully and intentionally made with such purpose grafted on your life.

Slow down. Slow your head so that you can feel your heart beat.

Stop running. Stop your head running through the why's, if's and how's.

Life is not going to pass you by. You are not going to miss out. Enjoy, oh enjoy. There is so much to taste, feel and see.

Maybe then you would realise how beautiful life is, stunning even.

You have so much to be grateful for in the here and now.

Go and adventure. Be brave. Don't be afraid to live. I mean really live. Awaken your heart and soul to adventure, hold nothing back.

Have conversations that matter. Let coffee dates linger in to dinner dates with no commitments awaiting you.

Fly to countries and experience cultures that allure your eye.

Take risks. Leap as far as your faith will take you.

Use this time to enjoy, experience and venture, but also use it to understand you.

Be vulnerable. Ask yourself the hard questions. Choose who you want to be.

Who do you want to be?

What do your values speak of?

What will you stand for?

Be the real you – raw you. Find her. Embrace her. Love her.

Take courage, dear heart. Life will not pass you by.

Promise,

Me

CHAPTER TWENTY FIVE

You are an explorer

You are an explorer. We all are.

Whether you are quiet, shy, loud, bold or moody, we each have something innate inside us that desires adventure.

Imagine if noticing the little, random things in our world became our job description.

Wake up.

Notice!

Eat breakfast.

Notice!

Go to work.

Notice!

A heart expectant and open waiting to find something interesting, discovering our world like we have never seen it before. Meeting new friends in random ways. Simple details noticed that could change our whole direction.

Lately I have made the decision again to explore, find and document that which is beautiful in my everyday. A little something that I am grateful for. Hot water in the shower, a smile from a stranger, a beautiful shell on the beach.

I met my husband in the most normal of circumstances. He was sitting at the back of church, I went over to say hello to a friend and he introduced me.

I could have missed that very boring moment. I could give you all the reasons why we shouldn't have been friends or eventually lovers. He was much younger than me. He was a personal trainer obsessed with fitness. I was not. He spoke a different language. The list goes on.

Something adventurous happened though that changed our initial interaction.

I noticed.

He gave me a little clue and I listened. He said this; "My Ouma died in South Africa today, we share the same birthday and she was very special to me."

I listened. Then the next Sunday I simply said to him, "How are you? How are you feeling about your Ouma?"

He could not believe that I remembered?

As someone away from his family and friends to find someone noticing his situation was the most attractive quality he could have ever wanted in someone. Someone who noticed.

That is where our love story began.

Inconsequential moments that made the beginnings of a great friendship

Life is full of crazy moments of unexpected happenings. Some delightful and some terrifying. No matter how difficult your circumstance is today, there is always something to explore, an opportunity to be grateful for.

There is always someone to notice. There is always some detail for you to remember.

What is one small step you can take towards noticing something inconsequential that might be your key to unlock potential in the future?

Adventure is awaiting discovery.

"Well, it seems to me that the best relationships – the ones that last – are frequently the ones that are rooted in friendship. You know, one day you look at the person and you see something more than you did the night before. Like a switch has been flicked somewhere. And the person who was just a friend is ... suddenly the only person you can ever imagine yourself with."

Gillian Anderson

23. EXPLORE A LITTLE.

Set a date.

Start the day with a big breakfast at a cafe you love.
Then start your exploration.

You are an explorer.

Your mission is to document and observe the world around you as if you've never seen it before.

Take notes.

Collect things you find on your travels.

Catch a bus or a train.

Walk in and out of art galleries and museums.

Document your findings.

Notice patterns.

Copy.

Trace.

Focus on one thing at a time.

The most important part:

Record who you are drawn to.

You may just surprise yourself.

Dear single self,

The day I turned 40, the most amazing man proposed to me on a scenic flight over Albany, just two weeks after we started dating. Whirlwind romance!

I'm still 40 (just) and we've been married for six months. God is so completely faithful to give you the desires of your heart even though at times you wonder if you should give up on your dream of sharing your life with someone.

In the meantime don't delay your other dreams! Travel, learn new things and enjoy the people in your world. Be thankful for what you have. Focus on what you can give and be creative in blessing those around you, even when you're tired, stretched and feel alone. It will expand your heart and change your perspective.

Live life to the full – EVERY day! Sow your life into things that matter and love the ride. Laugh a lot! Notice when you stop laughing and do something that makes you happy!

Know that your future is secure and don't wish away the now – it's not a waste; it's preparation for your future.

Stay balanced, some of the things you think are important aren't. Your relationship with God is! Making time to spend time with family and friends is! Looking after you is! Working too many hours isn't! Pleasing others isn't.

Be the most magnificent YOU!

Learn patience. There were times I thought the wait was forever but then it ended ... unexpectedly! You may not be in control of the timeline but you can determine how you use every day so don't under-rate where you are, enjoy single-land while you're there.

Love,

Me

CHAPTER TWENTY SIX

You are fabulous

Whilst surfing the web last week, I read a quote online and the only thing I remember from the piece of writing was this question ...

"Does it make you feel fabulous?"

This morning started out as a normal Wednesday. A bite of cereal, a strong flat white, off to the shops to get some groceries.

When I got home, that question ran through my mind again.

"Does it make you feel fabulous?"

Then suddenly my whole wardrobe was on the floor after I had ripped pile after pile out of its dark cavity.

I looked at every piece of clothing and every pair of shoes and asked myself this question.

Does it make me feel fabulous?

I realised there were old t-shirts that had been relegated to the 'exercise in these' pile, I had trackies that had been placed in the 'wear them to bed in winter' pile and I had a little defining moment.

Why shouldn't I feel fabulous when I exercise?

Why shouldn't I feel fabulous as I climb into bed?

I had an "I would prefer to have a smaller wardrobe full of beautiful items, than an overflowing one with half-hearted items that are there because of obligation" aha moment.

Obligation because I got them on sale.

Obligation because a friend gave them to me.

Obligation because I once loved them, but they no longer make me smile.

What are you holding onto out of obligation?

One of the greatest ways we can feel lighter and more inspired is to simplify the spaces we reside in.

Every time I do it, I am amazed at how great I feel afterwards.

One of my friend's uncle and aunt lost their whole house in a fire yesterday. As they walked around the charcoaled remains, they realised that possessions really didn't mean that much to them, when all of them kept their lives and health intact.

Possessions don't define us.

Popular culture tells us that whoever dies with the most stuff wins! When we think about it logically, we know this is not true.

Today, those bathers that are chlorine stretched, those pants that are stained and those shoes that I love but are so uncomfortable are all now in wardrobe heaven.

And I feel fabulous because of it.

What makes you feel fabulous?

It may be a massage, it may be new makeup, it may be a time in prayer, it may be a new season's worth of clothes ...

Today do something that makes you feel worthwhile, noticed and valued.

Because you are fabulous.

"You know what's really, powerfully sexy? A sense of humour. A taste for adventure. A healthy glow. Hips to grab on to. Openness. Confidence. Humility. Appetite. Intuition. Smart-ass comebacks. Presence. A quick wit. Dirty jokes told by an innocent looking lady. A storyteller. A genius. A doctor. A new mother. A woman who realises how beautiful she is."

Courtney E. Martin

24. DANCE AROUND THE HOUSE NAKED.

Okay, I am sure I have lost most of you after this Yestember dare.

But come on, you know you want to.

I don't mean you should do it in front of your random flatmates and I am encouraging you to make sure that all the curtains are shut.

Sometimes, though, we just need to throw caution to the wind and mix everything the hell up!

Mix it up.

You need to turn on some music.

You need to dance in your underwear if that feels more appropriate.

Mostly, you just need to celebrate your fabulous you.

Dance it out.

I promise you will feel absolutely ridiculous in the moment, but the little glint in your eye will sparkle because you have done something so reckless.

Hello hot stuff,

I can't tell you enough how valuable you are to the world ... single or married. Neither of those status should ever define you. But since our culture does tend to put us in boxes, let me share with you a few tips on how to live outside of any box that tries to confine you.

1. Be true to yourself. Go where you feel free. Do what makes you feel alive. Take risks that are just and true and scare yourself a little in stepping into that void. If you're taking actions in the pursuit of what is true, beautiful and just, you will always land on your feet – or at least fall into a net of feathers that makes you no worse off for the experience.

2. Discover my friend Jesus Christ and go on an international mission trip before you turn 21. Putting yourself in a situation where you are forced to trust him in a foreign land allows you the privilege of seeing first hand how great God is, how much he cares for our every need and He will give you an adventure you will never forget. Seeing this side of life through youthful eyes will set you up with a heart of compassion and an appreciation for humanity outside of our understanding. You will be blessed and changed forever. My tip is to make all of your holidays with a deeper purpose and you'll get way more value for your investment.

3. Beauty tips: Laugh a lot and stay young at heart – it makes you even look younger.

A. Cherish your sleep but not too much. I still think sleep ins are over rated and often a waste of a beautiful day of opportunity but some days you need to fill up your sleep tank. Value sleep enough to make sure you get a healthy amount of it, because there will be a time in the future you can't get enough.

B. Never die your hair. Calculate the average amount that just ten of your friends spend on hair dye treatments and put it away in a savings account. Then go on a holiday to Hawaii or something. With the exception of an experimental bright red fringe streak, my hair is still the same colour I was born with and the seasons will change its shade anyway.

C. Moisturise morning and night all over your face, neck and décolletage Use upward strokes (away from gravity) and your don't need an expensive product. Just one that feels lovely with sunscreen in it (for day time) and smells sweet to you (for night). I once met a lady in her 80's who did this and her face skin was amazing – her neck on the other hand showed her age ... Not that that's a bad thing either. ;)

D. Don't spray perfume where the sun can see – there's something in it that attacks freckles. Go old school and apply behind ears and wrists. Pick a scent you love and stick with it – people will remember that's your sweet fragrance years down the track.

E. Exercise. Find some kind of team sport or exercise you love, develop a passion for it and never stop playing (unless injury prevents of course). Use the sport as a tool when you find yourself in a new city to make new friends. It's worked for me every time.

F. Request pearls for a milestone birthday and wear them as often as you can – even with T-shirts. You can pass these on one day and they are classic and never go out of fashion. Never forget that beauty comes from within and let these pearls remind you of that.

4. Don't be in a rush to get married. There are so many great opportunities life can throw at you when it's just you. Don't shy away from these. Plan a world trip by couch surfing with friends (my 30th birthday present to myself).

5. Sex outside of marriage is over rated. Save it for the man you've married and you'll never regret it. There's a reason the Bible advised this too, so nestle up to a man of integrity, who shares this value and wait. Believe me there are guys out there like this and you only need one ... the right one.

6. Relationships are over rated until you're ready to get hitched and have kids. This is not to say don't go on the occasional date if asked by a worthy suitor, but don't force the issue or wish it to happen. It sounds cheesy but your heart is a valuable commodity and you don't want to waste it. To make this clearer – imagine if you had a sack of ten gold bars for the value of your heart for your lifetime. If you gave one of these gold bars away every time you got into a 'relationship' you might get to the point where you've met the man of your dreams but only had one or two left to offer him. Might be a bad analogy but you get the point.

7. Never ever ask a guy out (wait for him to ask you) and if he's far away – let him come to you. The times I made myself 'available' by being in their town – I always came away feeling like a git. The right one will come to you.

8. Start a charity that has longevity and sustainability. Not only can single people can start charities but it's definitely easier to do so without the pressure of the needs of husband and kids.

9. On issues of study, career and relationships, listen to advice from your family but still go with your gut. Your family loves you so wouldn't advise you without wanting what's best for you, but ultimately it's your life and you have to be strong enough to make your own decisions and then own them.

10. Create steady financial habits for your life and stick to them as soon as you get your first job. I wish I had, especially when I was single. No-one wants to be a budget nerd but peers will respect you for it and you might inspire others. Stealthily budget your living expenses without being over the top, and allocate funds for travel and savings and the things that matter to you. This will surprisingly give you more financial freedom than restriction. Trust me! And don't get a credit card! You don't need it. If you need extra cash – bank loan.

11. When you get married, your life is no longer your own. You share it. Your attention is not just on your needs but divided. And then if you have kids its divided again. There are definitely perks to marriage, but it also means you have to be prepared to check all those desires you had at the marriage door. So while you're single – live your life well. Dream large and make it happen. Walt Disney said, 'if you can dream it, you can do it' and don't wish to be put in a box of what people expect you should be doing by a certain age. On that note – feel free to watch cartoons and animated movies well into adulthood. It keeps your mind playful and will help if you have kids.

12. If your favourite song comes on in the grocery store – feel free to dance with the trolley. It's very liberating. Also run outside and dance in the rain every so often ... it's like dancing in the dew of God's goodness and grace. Can't imagine life without His saving grace. We need it single or married!

Whether you're single or married, savour life and enjoy loving HIM and others – the people God has put in front of you. There's so much more satisfaction in that!

Love Me.

CHAPTER TWENTY SEVEN

I feel safe now...

When we start to live a life of adventure, we step into places that make us uncomfortable but truly alive.

Recently I went on an adventure with my little family of four. A new playground, a much needed coffee, I wasn't expecting a very simple story to enter my normal.

As we got off the train at Leederville station, I noticed a young woman standing full of fear at the bottom of the ramp.

I stood behind her waiting for her to start her journey upwards.

She looked at me and simply said, "Go ahead of me, I am afraid of heights."

I said to her, "That's okay, do you want to hold my hand and we can walk the bridge together?"

You see, this particular ramp off the train station at Leederville connects to a bridge that takes you across a four-lane highway.

My truck, train, bus, ambulance, helicopter, plane, car, anything-that-moves toddler thinks this bridge is absolutely brilliant, but for the fearful of heights I can see this would be the Mount Everest of all bridges.

So there I was, at midday, walking across a bridge holding hands with a stranger. As we got closer to the end of the short journey, she turned to me and said simply, "I feel safe now."

We had spoken less than twenty words to each other. Held hands simply and then I let go of her hand and she walked off to find her friends.

This young woman had Downs syndrome and her tenacity at facing her fears and acknowledging her needs to a stranger was a profound lesson in trust to me.

How often do we need help but are afraid to admit it?

I was thinking about this simple story a few days later and it made me think of my relationship with God.

How much easier would have my single years been, if I just trusted him?

What if I said, "God, I feel afraid, will you walk beside me?"

"He rescued Israel from their oppressors = his love never quits.

Took Israel in hand with his powerful hand = his love never quits.

Split the red sea right in half = his love never quits.

Led Israel right down the middle = his love never quits."

Psalm 136: 10 – 13

No matter what we are going through, no matter the fears we face, no matter the largeness of the journey we must endure, His love will never fail us.

He delights in us,

He fights for us,

He remembers us,

He cares for us,

His love never quits.

He longs to hear us say "I feel safe now, so He can let go of our hand and release us into our new season."

25. TALK TO FIVE STRANGERS

It seems a little silly, but the hardest part to starting a conversation with a stranger is the first thirty seconds.

What if you just needed some practise at meeting new people?

What if a brilliant friendship was on the other side of all that awkwardness?

This is my Yestember challenge for you today.

Go and find five strangers and start up a decent conversation.

I mean a conversation that is beyond shallow.

Start a conversation with strangers and make it less awkward to meet new and interesting people.

Dear single self,

I am now 36 and I got married at 24.

Firstly I want to tell you of two books that changed my perspective on life and massively helped shape who I have become today. 'Who I am in Christ' by Neil Anderson and 'Love your Life' by Victoria Osteen.

To understand the revelation of knowing who you are in Christ is life-changing. It is not what you do that determines who you are. It is who you are that determines what you do.

And you, my young self are royalty! A true daughter of the most high king.

You have the right to live boldly with confidence!

Learn how to love unconditionally even though what you are going through doesn't seem fair.

Your need for acceptance and belonging are legitimate needs but don't attempt to meet them without God. Don't go looking for love in the wrong places. It will only bring much heartache and confusion. Stop trying to figure everything out, don't worry, God has your back!

Please don't wait too long to meet Jesus. He is on your side. He is your friend. He has a sense of humour!

He chose you, Yes, CHOSE YOU for great things. You are someone of great value and significance. He has your life mapped out with great surprises. An amazing husband and two children await you. There is no need to worry about what your future holds. Just focus on your relationship with Jesus. He is your encouragement, especially in those times you feel alone and unworthy.

You have a gift of writing. Start now! Write your thoughts, your troubles, your inspirations.

I pray that your eyes would be opened so that you may know and personally receive unconditional love and acceptance.

Don't compromise your faith, you are worth far more than gold.

Loving yourself is the greatest gift I can give you because you can't give away what you don't already have.

Get into the habit of speaking positive words over your life because a healthy self image will be one of your greatest assets. It will cause you to rise higher and inspire others to live at their best.

Life is not about waiting or putting things off until you've 'got it together' or until you've found 'the right one'. Start living now, don't hold back. Don't believe the negative spoken over you. You have the power and the authority to become the best 'You' you can be with God.

I love you,

Me

CHAPTER TWENTY EIGHT

Words

I am a words person through and through. There is something about the power of words spoken that bring life into my days but also bring fear, condemnation and strife as well.

Recently I spent the day with tea, a storm, a great friend and a two-year-old. The sun may have been hiding behind the clouds, but one thing we were not short of was a supply of words.

Simple story telling words,

Deep wisdom filled words,

Funny tale type of words,

Dreaming kind of words,

Encouragement into our future kind of words.

We spoke for hours on end and I promise you there was not one word spoken about another in comparison. There was not one word spoken that pulled other people down or comparison masked as helping another.

We spoke words of life.

There is nothing more discouraging for me than to walk away from a conversation full of gossip, talking about others and tearing people apart.

I honestly hate it. It leaves me feeling dirty. I am no saint.

I need to count the cost of my words often.

How is the tone of your words?

Do you find yourself telling everyone you meet, that there are just no guys?

Do you speak negatively about the season you find yourself in?

I am encouraging us to tell the truth but at the same time measure what we are speaking life into.

Let us be a people that choose our words carefully.

They bring life or death.
"Words kill, words give life;
They're either poison or fruit.
You choose."

Proverb 18: 21

26. BUY A DOUBLE PASS...

Your challenge today is to buy a double pass to a movie, a theatre show or a sports match.

Choose something and put it up on social media (Instagram, Facebook or the like) that you have a spare ticket going, who would like to come.

A simple challenge that is all about taking time to socialise first and foremost instead of spending another night in front of Netflix.

Mostly though, it is about stretching your frame of reference and opening yourself up to situations that may be uncomfortable.

Hanging out with someone does not mean a marriage proposal.

Stop thinking a date equals future. A date is just that. A space of time that you have booked in your calendar to hang out with somebody else.

Full stop.

"A lady's imagination is very rapid; it jumps from admiration to love, from love to matrimony in a moment."

Jane Austen, Pride and Prejudice

Dear Former Single Self,

I am now 31 and I was married at 28.

You may not know this now but guys that matter do not care what brand your handbag is. Nor do they care for a face full of make up or a fake tan (in fact, I have since discovered how much they hate those smells!). Great guys, guys worth your time, want you! They want to hang out with you, they want to know the real you, flaws and all! These are men worth investing your time in. Stop fantasising about what your 'husband' will look like and what he will do and be and blah blah blah ... Be you! That's the person people want to meet! Your flaws and quirks are what make you, you! These are the things that attract people to you, not the perfect version of you ... Snore!

I have learnt that what I perceived to be important to me in a man was actually wrong. Who I thought was my 'type' was a warped view that was dictated to me by media, music and friends. When I sit and look back, I realise I looked in the wrong places for the things I knew I wanted deep down. I wanted unconditional love, support for the times I can't do it on my own, encouragement when I'm unsure and, most of all, a best friend who I get to keep for the rest of my life! That's a man, that's a husband, that is someone who is worthy of investing my time in and getting to know. That's my husband, my best friend, my unconditional love!

Being single is actually great! Embrace it. Stop thinking there's something wrong with you, your time is coming! When people ask why you don't have a boyfriend, don't shy away with embarrassment. Own it! Open your eyes to the things around you, look up, look around. Befriend people, say yes more, get off your phone, get off your computer, interact with humans regardless of social status, popularity, music choice, fashion sense. (Trust me, my husband and I couldn't be further apart when it comes to music choice) You never know who you might meet, God has a plan and it's better than yours!

Stop moping about and fire up; you don't want to miss what's coming!

Me

CHAPTER TWENTY NINE

Admiration

Admiration brings with it a beautiful opportunity in a world full of so much judgement. I admire people for many different reasons ...

Mostly silently whilst I walk the shops, times when I sit and watch a documentary, sometimes at the beach as someone walks past slowly.

I admire single parents. I cannot imagine the late nights, alone with a sick child, those times when there is no-one to hold your hand, when you wait for answers from the doctors. I admire your tenacity, I admire how you keep going. I admire the two jobs you juggle just to make ends meet. If you are a single parent, I have never judged or discounted your opinion, I admire every single part of your being.

I admire people over eighty. Even when they are a little cranky, I kind of like it. They have so much perspective to give. I ask my grandmother questions all the time. Most responses come with a roll of her eyes, but I know secretly she loves it and, even more than that, I know she appreciates my attention. I especially love watching old people in love. It does something to my soul that I cannot explain. Seeing an elderly man grab the hand of his silver haired lover makes my heart race with romance and hope for the future.

I admire people who spend their days with young people at risk. People who take a chance on a young adult, who has attitude to boot and opinions bigger than the bell tower. I admire youth workers, youth chaplains, youth pastors, youth leaders, youth juvenile officers, social workers.

I admire cleaners. I watch and thank janitors, rubbish men and food hall cleaners all the time. I appreciate their attention to detail. I appreciate how hard they work for their families. I am humbled by their selflessness in taking time to serve another. Whether they are paid or not, I think they are the salt of the earth. Our country is blessed with the beauty of cleanliness, because someone cared enough to take away our over-abundance of rubbish. The event managers, the programme coordinators, the production personnel, all the people who create beautiful environments that we enjoy so often without contributing to their efforts.

I admire those in our community who overcome insurmountable odds. The mothers and fathers who have had sick children long-term, the parents who were once orphaned but now raise a family with pride. The visually impaired, the hearing challenged, those who have lost limbs, those who have been in tragic accidents. I admire tenacity. I admire pure grit. I admire an overweight person jogging down our beach. I admire people who wear their bikinis with pride after a mastectomy. I admire the depth of the human spirit, to dig deep and push through even when it hurts. I admire people who don't play the victim but get help and move past the tragedies that have ensnared them.

I admire the everyday person who is honest. Who tells the truth. Who isn't trying to be something they are not.

I admire the person who says sorry, who owns their part to play in the breakdown of relationship, who restores, forgives and trusts again.

I admire anyone who has been hurt in love, who loves again.

I admire kind humans. The person who believes the best and loves deeply.

If you are any of these things, it is quite possible I have spent time thinking about how amazing I think you are.

Maybe you have been framing yourself and your current season by what you don't have rather than the amazing tenacity and brilliance you inspire in others.

Re-framing who we admire and why, gives us a great opportunity to remind ourselves of what we are passionate about.

People with stories.

People with scars.

People with pasts.

They make the most interesting of companions.

27. WHAT DO YOU ADMIRE?

Maybe the list of things you have been looking for in a spouse are completely removed from the things you admire in human kind.

One of the greatest traits we can have in a marriage is mutual respect.

Respect goes way beyond an initial spark of attraction and someone's physical appearance. It is founded in admiration.

Draw a person.

Now brainstorm around that picture the things you admire most in people.

Remind yourself of these things when you are meeting new people and branching out on new opportunities.

The greatest relationships are founded in respect and admiration.

"Sexiness wears thin after a while and beauty fades, but to be married to a man who makes you laugh every day, ah, now that's a real treat."

Joanne Woodward

Dear single self,

How do I even begin to talk to you about the things that have radically changed my perspective of singleness. I am now nearly 38 and I got married when I was 34.

I want to tell you to stop worrying. Stop striving, stop wishing, stop craving, stop manipulating. I want to tell you to let go. Let go of all of those expectations, those overwhelming sessions of late night worrying, those times when you are so consumed with being single, that you have stopped living the life you are living.

You will get married one day.

You will have a child one day.

You will.

If only you could take hold of that truth and walk out this amazing season of your life with that perspective.
Enjoy yourself!

Hang out with guys without imaging what your wedding could be like to each other.

Stop fantasising and start living. You are loved and worthy of love. You belong and are worthy of belonging.

Drink deep drinks of the love of God and live a life that surrenders to beautiful things and beautiful moments.

You don't need to wait till you're married to start truly living.

Say yes. Say yes to beautiful, interesting things.

Live an interesting life.

Live large.

Love Me

(a very pregnant, very in love, very stretched, very tired but very satisfied me.)

CHAPTER THIRTY

Letting go

One of the greatest beginnings of any relationship is friendship. The problem is that technology, busy-ness, un-forgiveness and the age we live in have all made it so awkward to work out how to be a good friend. There is always a time for everything and sometimes friendships change, meaning it is time to transition.

How are you going in the changing seasons of friendships in your world?

Are you bitter and angry at all the friends who have become wives and mothers?

Do you find yourself alone, because everyone in your circle has walked the aisle?

I love summer, the long nights, the beach walks, the brilliant sunsets, the days spent swimming. Although summer makes me smile, I love winter as well. The crochet, the open fires, the slippers, hot water bottles, deep breaths in the morning that fill your lungs with freshness. Winter.

The darker months at my beach shack can be just as enchanting as the hotter ones. Some winters we have spent more days at the beach than our summers. The sun is less brutal, the wind is less fierce and winter is a little more forgiving here.

Personally, I don't struggle to let go of physical seasons. I love autumn with its colours. I adore Spring, its potential. Every season woos me with its beauty.

I do struggle to let go of seasons of friendship however. I grapple to know when the season asks me to dig deep and hold on. Then I wonder whether the time is asking me to give up gracefully. I have kind of always been a super loyal person, who believes that everyone can be and should be friends over decades rather than years. I struggle to give up on people. I see the best. I ignore the unmet phone calls. I love deeply.

The older I get though, the more I realise that the best of companions on the journey are the ones who embrace the season you find yourself in and not try to take you out of it. They take note of the season, they celebrate it and not try to remove you from it and sometimes people are just unable to go the distance, and that is okay.

The season I am currently in is so different to my former one. If I continually tried to be the person I was a few seasons ago, I would not be able to plant myself and grow in the place where I currently find myself. I would miss the moments, I would escape the kisses in the early morning hours (even though 4am cannot possibly ever be legal!), I would let someone else raise my babes.

One of the best gifts we can give our friends is acknowledgement of their current season. Reminding them to keep moving forward and not get stuck in places they were not designed to remain in.

This whole year, I have been saying over and over to myself, 'New Days, New Ways.' I want to be a friend who is aware of the new in my closest friends' seasons and encourage it, embrace it, even applaud it.

Let's not be the kind of friends that compete and compare, holding each other captive in a season that has past. Let's move forward into the new and embrace the tone of the season. Personally and corporately, together.

One of my favourite poems is from the book of Ecclesiastes ...

"There is a time for everything,
and a season for every activity under the heavens:
a time to be born and a time to die,
a time to plant and a time to uproot,
a time to kill and a time to heal,
a time to tear down and a time to build,
a time to weep and a time to laugh,
a time to mourn and a time to dance,
a time to scatter stones and a time to gather them,
a time to embrace and a time to refrain from embracing,
a time to search and a time to give up,
a time to keep and a time to throw away,
a time to tear and a time to mend,
a time to be silent and a time to speak,
a time to love and a time to hate,
a time for war and a time for peace."

Ecclesiastes 3:1-8 (NIV)

What is your current season and what do you need to let go of?

28. VOLUNTEER SOMEWHERE.

I was talking to my cousin recently and she was telling me how she had just joined our local theatre group. She is nearly forty and starting a new volunteering activity at her age is such a brilliant opportunity.

One of the best ways to meet new people is by volunteering somewhere.

Doing something together is one of the best ways to make new friends.

Where can you volunteer?

At a local soup kitchen.

A theatre company.

A library reading books to children.

A sports team coaching.

A church programme visiting the elderly.

Go on a trip overseas helping in an orphanage.

The opportunities are endless.

Take time to enrol to volunteer in the community today; you never know who is hanging out just waiting for a new friend.

CHAPTER THIRTY ONE

A massage on the inside

Recently, whilst on holiday, I did some Pilates and yoga classes. One morning, I ran out of my room so I could grab a coffee on my way to class and then settled into a session with the most patient and kindest teacher I have each ever encountered.

Actually she glowed. She was so peaceful and that was the most attractive quality. But to be truthful, she was very plain.

Plain in a good way; simple, honest, authentic, encouraging. She wasn't asking for attention or demanding our presence. She was soft, graceful and forgiving.

As we began the class, I took a deep breath and thought about simple things that make people really attractive. Two pregnancies in three years have really taken their toll on my body and I am really determined to find ways to rediscover my strength again. More than a physical overhaul, I really need to find a way to accept myself, my body and find my peace in the midst of that.

We moved into the routines and, in the middle of a pose, she said something that I had never even considered before. It was the most perfect analogy for where I am at creatively and also in my novice motherhood. She said this; "Breathing is like a massage for your insides."

Such a simple thought that made me realise why I found her so peaceful. She took time to find her peace and centre through breathing and exercises that were her foundation.

My body holds stresses in specific places and as I breathe intentionally the relaxing of my whole countenance makes me a more approachable person.

A deep breath.

A long breath.

It is a gift that we give to ourselves.

The art of relaxation can be founded on this simple statement from my instructor.

A silly little thought in some ways, but extremely liberating in the art of letting go and allowing peace to reign.

Are you struggling to relax?

Do you find anxiety is replacing peace in your days?

Why don't you start with the basics, with me and take a deep breath and remember the simple things that you are grateful for.

Find a way to dig deep and give yourself a massage on the insides.

29. BREATHE DEEP.

Today's challenge is to go to a Pilates, body balance or yoga class.

Going to a new exercise class and taking time to prefer our health and well being is an amazing way to look after yourself.

A deep breath.

A stretch and release.

Opportunities to forgive.

Moments of gratefulness.

You won't regret this and your body will smile from the inside out.

Dear single self,

You got married way younger than you ever expected or planned to, but when he came along, he messed up all of your plans in the most perfect way.

You may not know this now, but that dream you've been holding quietly in your heart for so long, you make it happen. He's the reason you get the ball rolling in the first place, and you're the reason he gets his ideas off the ground too.

I have learnt that you can't do everything well. So you should give up trying because it's exhausting! Find those few things you absolutely love. Those things that breathe life. Those things that you couldn't imagine your life without. And do those well.

You will never guess how you're going to struggle. How sick you will be. How debilitating it will be. But how, in the midst of that, you'll begin to grow into the person you know deep down that you're meant to be. You'll never guess how messy life is, or how out of control you will feel. But you'll also never guess how content you will be when you do what it is that you're meant to be doing, with the person you're meant to be doing it with.

Everyone will tell you that the first year of marriage is the hardest, but in your case, they're dead wrong. Even with serious health and financial stress, it's one of the best years of your life.

Follow your gut.

Because you find him.

And when you know, you know.

Love,

Me

(I am now 24 and I was married at 21.)

CHAPTER THIRTY TWO

You are not too old

Lately I have had a few conversations that have ended with the statement, "Oh maybe I am just getting a little old for that."

Who told you that?

My grandmother is ninety one and she honestly is the bravest woman I know. Yes she is legally blind but she lives alone in an apartment, she travels an hour every Tuesday for a mosaic class and she went to Bali in August for a holiday.

I asked her, "Grandma, what was your favourite part of the trip?" She said with a cheeky grin, "I had a massage every single day!"

A quote I read this week inspired me;

> *"Breathe my friend, you are not old. You are young. You are not a mess, you are normal. Extraordinary perhaps. In the blink of an eye your life will change and it will continue to change for decades to come. Enjoy it. Embrace it ... Be grateful for the ride. You are not too old. You are young. And faith will get you everywhere. Just you wait."*
>
> *Abby Larson*

I have found the older I get, the more hesitant I am in trying something new. I thought it would be the other way round, because I thought the older I got, the braver I would be. I hoped that I would have learnt that people come and go, life keeps moving on and in the end those things that worried me just don't really matter any more.

As I gain perspective and chat with friends who are living brave no matter their age, I decide that I want to do it a little different. I am determined to start forgetting my age and living the life I want to. Deciding to live in the moment, trusting my journey and taking brave steps towards new and glorious opportunities.

The funny thing about today is this ...

You are today the youngest you will ever be and also today you are the oldest you have ever been. So if you think about this moment right now and those dreams you have been putting off because of an age problem, it doesn't really make any sense.

If you think you are too young for something today ...

Maybe you're not.

If you think you are too old today to start living the life you have always dreamed of ...

Who said so?

Dream that dream.

Buy that dress.

Throw out that box.

Book that holiday.

Phone that friend.

Let go of that offence.

Date that man ... even if it is a little awkward.

Today.

I promise you are not too old.

You are never too old to begin again.

"You are not too old and it is not too late to dive into your increasing depths where life calmly gives out its own secret."

Rainer Rilke

30. RECAP: WHAT HAVE YOU MISSED?

Go back through all the Yestember dares and see what you have missed.

One may jump out at you.

One you just couldn't complete back then but now you can.

Look for any patterns that are reoccurring that may be limiting you.

After you have looked through all your dares and your responses to them, write this sentence in your journal:

"I am not old to ..."

What is the first thing that comes to mind?

Don't over think it.

What has been taunting you in your subconscious?

You are not too old.

I promise.

Make steps towards finding freedom from that fear and step towards your new day.

YESTEMBER DARE

Checklist

- ☐ SAY YES
- ☐ BUY A COFFEE FOR A STRANGER
- ☐ WRITE A LETTER TO YOURSELF
- ☐ COOK A RECIPE YOU HAVE NEVER COOKED BEFORE
- ☐ ARRANGE DINNER IN THE CITY WITH A GROUP OF PEOPLE
- ☐ GO SPEND TIME ALONE, SOMEWHERE IN NATURE
- ☐ TAKE A HEART EXAMINATION?
- ☐ HAVE A COFFEE WITH A PENSIONER
- ☐ WRITE A MESSAGE ON A MIRROR
- ☐ JIGSAW PUZZLE TIME
- ☐ BOOK A COUNSELLING SESSION
- ☐ CLEAN SOMEONE'S HOUSE
- ☐ GO TO THE MOVIES BY YOURSELF
- ☐ START A JOURNAL FOR YOUR FUTURE HUSBAND
- ☐ BUY A PACKET OF CRAYONS AND COLOUR IN
- ☐ WRITE A LIST OF WHAT MAKES YOU FEEL MOST CONNECTED
- ☐ BOOK A HOLIDAY
- ☐ CAFE CONVERSATION: SELF CARE
- ☐ WHAT HAVE YOU BEEN WAITING FOR?
- ☐ OBLIGATIONS VERSUS OPPORTUNITY
- ☐ EXPLORE A LITTLE
- ☐ DANCE AROUND THE HOUSE NAKED
- ☐ TALK TO FIVE STRANGERS
- ☐ BUY A DOUBLE PASS
- ☐ WHAT DO YOU ADMIRE?
- ☐ VOLUNTEER SOMEWHERE
- ☐ BREATHE DEEP
- ☐ RECAP: WHAT HAVE YOU MISSED?

Dear single self,

You have always wanted to be married and have children. It has been a dream since you were a little girl. I know you thought by now that you would be married. Forty six and very single, with no children. It's okay, I can see that you are waiting well.

A lot has happened in your life like when you were involved in a car accident in 2004. So much pain, a lot of muscle injury and it was so frustrating that you weren't allowed to go back to work.

Remember those years when you sank into a very dangerous level of anorexia.

You are probably thinking what has this to do with being single? Well, it led you to find out who you really are, discovering your purpose, desires and goals. Out of the hardest part of your life, you learned to live and dream again.

If you had met a man before this season, you know that you would have become an extension of Him and not really discovered your worth. You would have never discovered that you are brave, that you love helping people and started to live beyond those years of pain.

Today your life is so full and I can see that in this season you are brave and waiting well. Your faith sustains you, God restores your dreams and he has the right man for you at the right time. Your faith that God has a plan and a purpose for your life is inspiring.

Does that mean you should just wait around for your future husband to arrive, looking longingly out the window? – no!

While you are waiting, explore and keep trying new things. Remember your great friend and mentor who challenged you last year to say yes to things. Don't forget how much this tested you and allowed new experiences and amazing adventures.

Your dream of becoming a primary school chaplain has been the most amazing fulfilment of great promises and your life is so much bigger than you could have ever imagined. You help children to grow and discover themselves. You help families in times of crisis and you are the most amazing aunty to your family.

Don't give up, a lot can happen in a year.

You are divine no matter what age, God has not given up on you yet,

Waiting well, Me.

CHAPTER THIRTY THREE

Epilogue

As I sit here reflecting on what I really want to leave you with, I am overwhelmed at the complexity. As you can see from every story documented in the Letters to our single selves through this book, every person's story is so completely unique.

There is no formula.

There is no quick fix.

The only thing I know for sure is that there is hope.

I have rifled through twenty years of my journals searching for something, some little revelation that would do justice to the empathy I feel towards you, my reader.

I don't feel sorry for you, I don't pity you.

I just understand the season of in-between well and remember the times that I waited with my heart in my hand, quivering softly.

I just discovered this scripture that I had highlighted in my scrappy journal eighteen years ago. It said this in bold, messy writing:

> *"I will surely bless you and give you many descendants. And so after waiting patiently, Abraham received what was promised."*
>
> *Hebrews 6: 14-15 (NIV)*

Another scripture that sustained me through years of heartache and pain was this one from the Song of Solomon:

"Do not arouse or awaken love until it so desires."

Song of Songs 8:4

I used to write this scripture over and over until I believed and found hope in the potential that there was actually a due time.

These are just little reminders that God gave me along the way, that he was present and at work to bring all things together for good.

He taught me lessons, He sang over me with his love, He showed me that He was faithful, even in seasons when I didn't believe that He was even present.

The greatest place we can stay in is a position of promise. A place where our heart is engaged in hope, waiting and trusting that He sees and knows us.

That before the earth was formed, He knew us, He formed us in our mother's womb and every day, before any of them even came to pass, He had designed and seen.

He knows us.

He hears us.

Sometimes he just is a little slow on the uptake.

But He, in the end, is the author that I trust and know seasons of waiting will come again.

Seasons when I will need to search deeply and face the true essence of who I am, dig deep and say

Dear self,

Tomorrow is another day.

Don't give up.

Don't lose hope.

You never know,

A lot can happen in a year.

Love,

Me.

A letter to my daughter Liberty...

Dear Liberty,

Today you are all of seven months old and crawling around my feet, but I know this will go quickly, so I wanted to take time today to write.

Hoping you won't ever forget. Hoping I don't forget. Hoping for your life that you will find your feet in a place that makes you feel more alive than the day you came screaming into this world.

My little girl, we have just come home from your first trip overseas and, as we walked through villages in eastern Bali, we encountered people who were spellbound with your beauty. They would tell me how pretty your blond hair was and would ask if they could hold you. They were enchanted by your blue eyes, telling me how bright and clear they were.

As much as I think you are utterly scrumptious, I have travelled enough to know that they love you because, in their eyes and experience, you are extremely rare and unique. Different. What makes me terribly sad is knowing that there are products lining Asian supermarkets promising to make skin whiter and contact lenses available everywhere to turn their eyes blue.

This is the one thing about humanity and especially being a woman that I find so deeply disturbing. We are all unique and beautiful in so many different ways. Yet we spend our money and days trying desperately to be accepted. We change our appearance to look like everyone else. From surgery to extreme practices, to diets and manipulations. We covet other women's lives and looks, then wonder why we are so unhappy.

My prayer for you, my beautiful girl, is not that you would never feel the pain of regret and lessons learnt because these are the moments from which I have grown and learnt in the years that I have been graciously given.

My prayer is this...

That you would find the absolute brilliance in being you.

That you would discover the women who fought so many years ago so you can vote and not take that gift for granted.

That you may put on your football boots like your cousin Charlotte and run onto the oval, and then take them off, put on your ballet shoes and run off to class all in the one day. If that is how you want to spend your Saturdays.

That you would never look at another woman and envy the way she looks. Comparing and competing the uniqueness of her skin and shape.

That you would see people in your class at school who are different and think they are cool and interesting rather than weird and excluded.

My prayer is that you would change your world over and over, by finding out who you are and standing firm in that revelation.

I hope for all of this and so much more, but my greatest hope is this.

That you would find freedom as your namesake declares.

That your freedom as a woman would be girthed in every step that you take.

That you would know how many women and young girls around the world do not know the gift of freedom and fight everyday to just get by.

Women who are not allowed an education.

Little girls who are sold into jobs that even adults were not designed for.

People who scrounge around rubbish dumps to find something to put on their family's table.

Freedom is a gift my precious girl and I pray that you would continue to find it in your everyday, encouraging your friends to fight for it as well.

That diversity would not scare you.

That you would be a kind human.

That you would grow to accept differences in race, gender, religion and belief as something to be explored rather than shut down. Made fun of.

Find your unique, my dearest and then celebrate others in discovering what they were designed for as well.

Till we wake again tomorrow,

Love from your Mum,

Amanda

Thank You

Charl, Thank you for believing in me and constantly reminding me that together we can do anything. Every time you say yes, when my heart and mind quiver with maybe, you ignite that belief in my everyday.

Maximus and Liberty, you can never truly fathom how long I waited and prayed for your craziness.

My Family, all of you. Our extended tribe that goes on and on. Thank you for being my village.

Sarah, my editor in chief, all the way from London to Perth, our stories and emails, continue to fly and I'm so grateful that you listened in english grammar class, when I was off creating random stories in my imagination.

Kellie, my designer and chief cheerleader, this project remained in such a stagnated place until we had that simple dinner downtown Perth. I am so grateful for your generosity, encouragement and capacity to draw out dreams. I am sure this book would have remained on my desktop, taunting me if we had not taken the time to simply dream together. Thank you.

Kiri, my assistant. You came into my life in such a beautiful way. Thank you so much for saying yes.

Jo-Anne, my intern. Oh my goodness. We actually pulled this off. Those times with flat white in hand and email in flight, trying desperately to pull this project and the contributors together from all over the world. This my friend is what dreams are made of. I cant wait to read yours next.

My writing gang, you know who you are. The ones that encourage me, when I think I might turn off my computer. The ones that send out the prayer and love in the midst of testing times. Those who continue to write, even when we are sure no one is listening. You my friends are my greatest gift in this season. Karina, Elaine, Jodie, Em, Cate, Meg and the list continues on and on.

My Kinwomen. The group of women that stand around my life and encourage me to continue to find my voice, no matter the season or job title. Thank you for being the older and younger sisters I needed.

And lastly, but far from the least every single woman who took the time to write me a letter and share their story. I value you, I appreciate you and I am so grateful for your vulnerability. May every person who reads your truth, be inspired by your courage, tenacity and opportunity for perspective.

Printed in Australia
AUOC02n1815290117
282563AU00002B/2/P

9 781684 191727